PLC 2.0 Toolkit
Tools and Protocols For Observable Impact

Cale Birk and Garth Larson, Ed.D

Copyright 2019 by FIRST Educational Resources, LLC

All rights are reserved. No part of this publication may be reproduced in any form or by any electronic or mechanical means, including information storage and retrieval systems, without permission in writing by FIRST Educational Resources, LLC. For information regarding permissions, please contact FIRST Educational Resources, LLC at info@firsteducation-us.com.

Published by FIRST Educational Resources, LLC
Oshkosh, Wisconsin
www.firsteducation-us.com
info@firsteducation-us.com

Printed in the United States of America
(Steinert Printing Company, Oshkosh, WI)

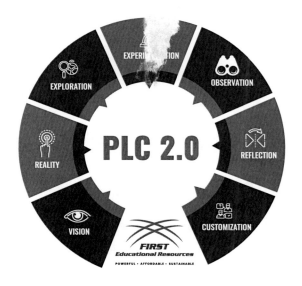

INTRODUCTION - WHY THE PLC 2.0 TOOLKIT?

> "The next big thing is the one that makes the last big thing usable."
>
> **Blake Ross**
> **Co-creator of Mozilla Firefox**

Welcome to the PLC 2.0 Toolkit, the companion book to *PLC 2.0: Collaborating for Observable Impact in Today's Schools*. If you are collaboratively exploring this PLC 2.0 Toolkit, we hope it is a result of our thoughts and ideas resonating from the first book. If you skipped the first book and wanted to jump into the Toolkit, that works too! Either way, we hope you find the tools and protocols in this easy to use booklet helpful in creating observable impact.

The PLC 2.0 Toolkit is designed to meet schools where they are at. Perhaps you are a district who is considering implementing teacher collaboration time into school timetables. You might be a school that has gotten the board approvals, agreement from the senior leadership team at the district office, staff consensus, community support, and you are excited to jump into collaboration. You could be at the stage where your school has had time for teachers to work together to examine their practice, and you are looking for some new ideas. You could be a collaborative leader who is busy, tired, and is looking for a bit of help to keep your team going.

Or you could be just plain frustrated: you had hoped that teacher collaboration would allow educators to get down to the business making a difference in making students the global-minded, critical and creative thinkers can thrive in an ever-changing world, but you have recently had a teacher ask if they could collaborate by themselves. Wherever you are at, we hear you!

As we referenced in *PLC 2.0: Collaborating for Observable Impact in Today's Schools*, educators across the globe have invested time, effort and resources into creating collaboration time with varying levels of success, failure, frustration, and elation, and nearly every other emotion in between. While the research on educators collaborating to examine and improve their practice is clear, the practice of educators working together and the impact this has on changing the learning experience for students is less conclusive. PLC 2.0 moves districts and schools beyond research to PRACTICE and more importantly to OBSERVABLE IMPACT—the type of impact that we can observe in our classrooms.

But getting to the impactful educator collaboration that makes a difference for the students in our classrooms is hard work, especially for teachers who are (rightfully) busy teaching! We have listened to educators all over the world share their struggles with collaboration: from challenges in determining what is most important for students to learn, to maintaining focus during collaborative time, to the pragmatic issues that can arise when leading the actual process of collaboration with busy and competent teachers who are as diverse as the students in their class! Repeatedly we heard a common theme from teachers and teacher leaders when it came to collaboration: "Sometimes, we just don't know what to do." The PLC 2.0 Toolkit has been designed to do two things: first, to provide user-friendly tools and protocols to help busy teachers and schools deepen the impact of their collaboration, and secondly to make that impact OBSERVABLE so that teachers can begin to reflect on their practice in a way that allows them to make connections between the teaching moves, activities and assessments they use in their classroom and their resulting impact on student learning.

Each tool that you will see in the PLC 2.0 Toolkit comes with an accompanying, step-by-step

PLC 2.0 Toolkit

protocol that helps guide team leaders and collaborative groups through their collaborative meetings. Each protocol has been designed to make the process of collaborative learning active, with routines and reflective processes that not only can be used by the team during the collaborative meeting, but by team members in their classrooms with students. If we can leave our meetings better able to connect our actions to impact AND have an activity that we can later use with our students, we have made teacher collaboration doubly meaningful. Furthermore, each tool is designed to be a visible and tangible artifact of team learning: in each of the protocols, collaborative teams are encouraged to make one of the tools a 'master copy' that can be attached to an Evidence Wall (see the 'Evidence Wall Protocol' later on in the Toolkit) to make collaborative team learning highly observable to the team itself and to any other interested visitors in the school.

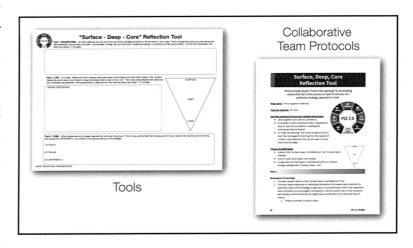

The tools and protocols in the PLC 2.0 Toolkit can be used 'as-is', or they can be modified to fit the individual needs of the team leader or collaborative team. If you wish to follow them step-by-step, that's great! If you have a variation that you have used that makes the tool more applicable to your context, even better! We see the tools and protocols much like a food service company; like 'Plated' might see their home-delivered, precisely-portioned recipes that are ready-to-cook: they guide us through the process of creating new and different meals with exciting flavors that we might not yet have tasted. For highly accomplished and experienced chefs, ready-to-cook meals provide us with support when we are busy or running behind, or even inspire us with unique combinations we might not have thought of. For those who are new to cooking, these 'mostly-prepared' meals allow us to have a level of comfort in experimenting with cooking without feeling the stress of wondering whether the meal is going to turn out. And as time passes, we gradually get better at determining the portions, flavors and methods that create the meals that appeal to our crowd. The PLC 2.0 tools are designed to meet the needs of experienced and less-experienced 'chefs': the collaborative team leaders in our schools. And if a collaborative meeting comes along and the team leader is away, no problem! Much like the meals from Plated, the PLC 2.0 tools can be picked up and facilitated by any team member.

This toolkit is designed to be differentiated for every school district, school, team, and educator. In *PLC 2.0: Collaborating for Observable Impact in Today's Schools*, we said that co-creating an observable vision of a learner, confronting our evidence based reality, and understanding the learning that we need to do as a collaborative team can seem overwhelming. Without question, to pick up this book and immediately follow each tool and protocol created in lock-step fashion would be not only be overwhelming, it likely would not be the ideal fit. Schools are actually much like the learners in our classes: they are diverse, they have strengths, they have challenges and they are at varying points on a developmental trajectory. So much like the approach to customizing learning for a student, the most valuable thing that any leader (whether they are the Superintendent, principal, school-based teacher or collaborative team leader) can do is to get the clearest, most high-resolution picture of their school or department as they possibly can.

We can start to co-design a customized approach to collaboration by looking for the strengths in a school and the educators, understanding how they learn best, and determining our prior knowledge and attitudes towards developing connections between their actions and the impact on student learning. For some of your schools, it may involve re-visiting your Vision of a Learner. For others, it might be taking a closer look at the design of the activities and assessments to make the products of learning visible. And still for others, it may just be looking at your professional development plan for next year and saying, "How are we going to know if this PD is going to make a difference?"

PLC 2.0 Toolkit

We need to uncover the honest, co-constructed answers to each of these questions:

- What's our co-created vision of a learner?
- What's our evidence-based reality?
- What's our learning that we need to do?
- What's our action and observable impact?
- What's our reflection?
- What's our customized support?

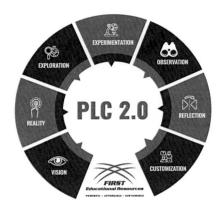

The key is the co-construction of the answers using the tools and protocols provided in this Toolkit. It cannot just be district or school leaders who are responding to these questions and creating more compliance in teams. It's all educators collaborating together with practical tools to create observable impact within our schools. Test the tools, use them as often or little as needed and more importantly, enjoy the collaborative journey in closing the gap between the co-created vision of a learner and the evidence-based reality in your context.

We hope you find these tools useful in creating collaboration with impact for your learners in this ever-changing world of education!

Table of Tools and Protocols

Evidence Wall Template This tool helps departments and grade level groupings develop a vision and team norms that enable team thinking and learning to be observable.	Pages 10-15
Vision of a Learner Protocol **(Part 1)** This tool helps school leaders, collaborative teams and partner groups co-create the attributes that will begin to comprise the Vision of a Learner.	Pages 16-20
Vision of a Learner Protocol **(Part 2)** This tool helps school leaders, collaborative teams and partner groups to de-construct the attributes to co-create an observable Vision of a Learner.	Pages 21-23
Vision To Outcomes Connector Tool This tool helps departments and grade level groupings connect their curriculum to their Vision of a Learner.	Pages 24-28
Vision To Collaborative Team **Connector Tool** This tool helps departments and grade level groupings develop a departmental-specific vision based on the School Vision of a Learner.	Pages 29-32
Vision To Task 'Feed-Forward' Tool This tool helps collaborative teams give "feed-forward" to each other as they connect their tasks and activities to their Vision of a Learner.	Pages 33-36
Illuminator Task/Assessment **Idea Generator** This tool sparks creative ideas and generate tasks and assessments that allow teachers to observe students DOING and DEMONSTRATING high-priority outcomes through the lens of the Vision of a Learner.	Pages 37-40

PLC 2.0 Toolkit

Balanced Assessment Profile Tool This tool helps collaborative teams create a balanced assessment plan through the lens of an attribute from the Vision of A Learner.	Pages 41-45
Activity/Assessment Analysis Tool This tool helps teams determine how the activities/assessments in an upcoming unit can be adapted to observe students demonstrating the Vision of a Learner.	Pages 46-50
Professional Learning For Observable Impact Tool This tool helps departments and grade level teams develop a research-based and "do-able" professional learning plan that can be assessed for its impact on classroom practice.	Pages 51-57
Support Structures (Part 1) **Preparing For Impact** This tool builds a creative thinking routine to co-design a vision of a high-impact learning support structures (staff meetings, collaborative meetings, PD days, etc.).	Pages 58-62
Support Structures (Part 2) **Reflecting On Impact** This tool helps staff reflect on the impact of learning support structures (staff meetings, collaborative meetings, PD days, etc.).	Pages 62-66
Rapid Research Jigsaw Tool This tool helps collaborative teams do a rapid research scan of a new strategy to determine if it has potential for positive impact on a learning challenge.	Pages 67-72
Attribute Analysis Tool **(At/Need To Go)** This tool helps collaborative teams to look at their current level of progress in an attribute area and prioritize their next steps.	Pages 73-79
Engaging Task Generator This tool helps collaborative teams create engaging, learner-centered tasks to help students learn our highest priority outcomes and demonstrate attributes of our Vision of a Learner.	Pages 80-84

Classroom Observation Tool This tool helps members of collaborative teams to prepare for effective, descriptive self- or peer-observations of an activity sequence or lesson.	Pages 85-89
Observation to Impact Connection Tool (Team) **(Post-observation)** This tool helps members of collaborative teams unpack classroom observations and connect their actions to impact in the classroom.	Pages 90-93
"Get To The Root" **Root Cause Analysis Tool** This post-observation tool helps teams move beyond "it worked" or "it didn't work" when collaboratively reflecting on a lesson, activity or approach.	Pages 94-97
Surface, Deep, Core Reflection Tool This tool helps teams "lock in the learning" by de-briefing causes that led to the success (or lack of success) of a particular strategy, approach or task.	Pages 98-100
Strategy Review This tool creates a departmental, "Trip Advisor-style" review of a strategy or approach to consolidate the team observations and learning from an impact cycle.	Pages 101-105
In Their Shoes Protocol This tool helps teams take an empathetic, student-centered approach to designing customized learning for students.	Pages 106-109
Individual Customization Plan This tool helps collaborative teams design a strengths-based, customized action plan to engage a learner in high-priority tasks.	Pages 110-118
Organizational Assessment Tool This tool helps school leaders and collaborative teams develop a baseline and track progress in each of the PLC 2.0 elements.	Pages 119-124

PLC 2.0 Toolkit
Tools and Protocols for Observable Impact

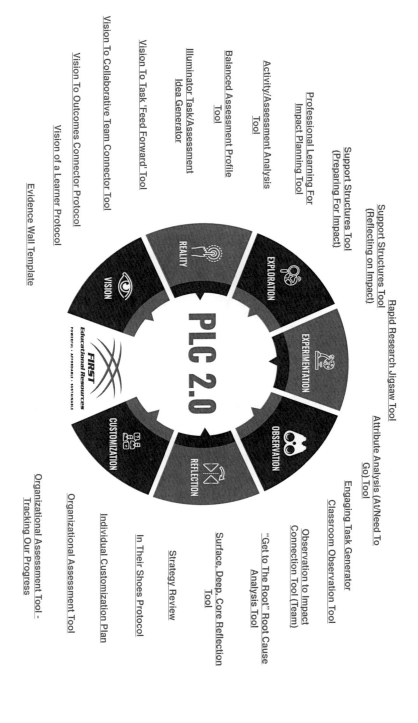

- Support Structures Tool (Reflecting on Impact)
- Rapid Research Jigsaw Tool
- Attribute Analysis (At/Need To Go) Tool
- Engaging Task Generator
- Classroom Observation Tool
- Observation to Impact Connection Tool (Team)
- "Get to The Root" Root Cause Analysis Tool
- Surface, Deep, Core Reflection Tool
- Strategy Review
- In Their Shoes Protocol
- Individual Customization Plan
- Organizational Assessment Tool
- Organizational Assessment Tool - Tracking Our Progress
- Evidence Wall Template
- Vision of a Learner Protocol
- Vision To Outcomes Connector Protocol
- Vision To Collaborative Team Connector Tool
- Vision To Task 'Feed Forward' Tool
- Illuminator Task/Assessment Idea Generator
- Balanced Assessment Profile Tool
- Activity/Assessment Analysis Tool
- Professional Learning For Impact Planning Tool
- Support Structures Tool (Preparing For Impact)

NOTE: Descriptions of each protocol are listed below starting at Evidence Wall Template/Protocol and going clockwise.

PLC 2.0 Toolkit

Evidence Wall Protocol

DEPARTMENT/COLLABORATIVE TEAM: _____

CROSS CONTEXT LEARNING

Inspiration Context: _____

Our Context

Less ← → More

Less ← → More

LEARN: What can we transfer from this context to our context to make the products of our collaborative learning observable to our team and to others?

ACTION: As a result of our learning, we will…

PLC 2.0 Toolkit

©FIRST EDUCATIONAL RESOURCES 2019

10

PLC 2.0 Evidence Wall Template (Sample)

©FIRST EDUCATIONAL RESOURCES 2019

"VISION IN OUR CONTEXT" (Department/ Collaborative Group)

"OUR REALITY"

"HOW WE KNOW"

"OUR LEARNING"

"OUR ACTION"

"OUR OBSERVABLE IMPACT"

"LEARNING FOR ALL OF US"

"CLOSING THE GAP"

SCHOOL-WIDE VISION OF A LEARNER <KEY ATTRIBUTES>

KEY ATTRIBUTE
< >
"Doing and Demonstrating"
— Task Analysis
— Assessment Analysis

ATTRIBUTE ASSESSMENT PROFILES
ILLUMINATOR TASKS / ASSESSMENTS

PROFESSIONAL LEARNING FOR IMPACT PLAN / SUPPORT STRUCTURES FOR IMPACT PLAN

"IF WE…THEN WE WILL OBSERVE…"

PROFESSIONAL LEARNING FOCUS AREA #1

PROFESSIONAL LEARNING FOCUS AREA #2

Impact Review
Design Observe

ATTRIBUTE ASSESSMENT PROFILES
ILLUMINATOR TASKS / ASSESSMENTS

CONNECTING OUR ACTIONS TO IMPACT
Connect - Reflect - Learn

STRATEGY REVIEW

CUSTOMIZATION PLAN

SCHOOL-WIDE VISION OF A LEARNER <KEY ATTRIBUTES>

PLC 2.0 Toolkit

11

Evidence Wall Protocol

This tool helps departments and grade level groupings develop a vision and team norms that enable team thinking and learning to be observable.

Prep time: 5 minutes to photocopy this protocol, a copy of the 'Evidence Wall Protocol', and to gather materials below

Time for Activity: 40-45 minutes

Use this protocol to have your collaborative team:
- develop a vision of a process to make their thinking visible in their context.
- develop norms to ensure that the products of collaboration are observable and helpful to the team.

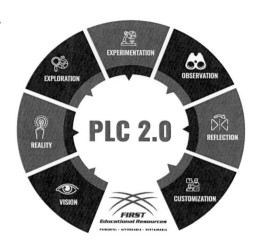

Things You Will Need:
- copies of this protocol for each participant
- Post-it notes, markers
- a large piece of chart paper attached to a vertical, flat surface in the collaborative area, divided in half by a dashed line, with one half labeled "Classroom" and the other labeled "Our Space" with an arrow at the bottom labeled "Less" and "More"

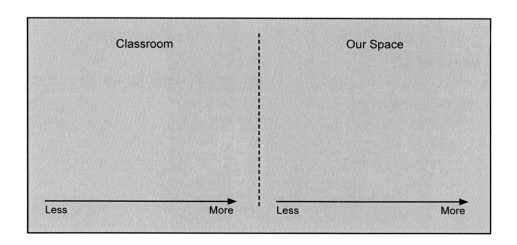

PLC 2.0 Toolkit

Part 1

Priming the Pump (10 minutes)

1. The team leader welcomes the group, and informs them of the purpose of the meeting and the learning targets for the group:
    a. "Today, we are going to be coming up with our team's answer to this question, 'How might we ensure that our collaborative team learning is evident to each of us on the team, and to anyone that came into this space, even if we weren't here?'"
2. The team leader then asks a priming question, "To get us started, if we were to walk into an empty kindergarten classroom one evening at the end of a term, what would we observe in that classroom that could inform us about what the students had learned over the term?"
    a. The team leader asks the team to silently reflect on the question and write down 4-6 things that they would observe on Post-It notes.
3. The team leader then asks each team member to prioritize their own Post-Its from "less informative" to "very informative."
4. The team leader then says, "Now, what I would like you to do is place your Post-It notes on the Classroom portion of the chart paper, ordering them horizontally from less informative on the left to more informative."
    a. The ones closest to the middle of the page should be the observations/artifacts that would be most informative to us in terms of what students would have learned in the kindergarten class.
5. Team members place their stickies on the Classroom portion of the chart paper.

Part 2

'Upticking' the Artifacts (5 minutes)

1. The team leader asks the team to look at the Post-It notes and see what they notice.
    a. "What are the things that are most informative? What makes them more informative?"
        i. The team looks for characteristics of the artifacts that best "speak for themselves."
    b. "What are the things that are LEAST informative? What makes them less informative?"
        i. The team looks for characteristics of the artifacts that aren't as able to speak for themselves.
2. The team then looks at each of the Post-It notes and comes up with at least one idea per Post-It note that would make that artifact more informative.

PLC 2.0 Toolkit

a. These "upticks" are written on the Post-It notes until each of them has been made better.

Part 3

Cross-Context Learning (20 minutes)

1. The team leader then asks, "Given what we would observe in this classroom and the upticks that we have made to each artifact, what can we learn from this classroom about making thinking and learning visible in our space?"

2. The team then examines each of the Post-It notes from the Classroom setting and begins to pull across those Post-Its that might best help the collaborative team space speak for itself.

   a. The ideas that are pulled across to the "Our Space" side are ordered in the same fashion: the ideas that would be most informative are placed on the "More" side of the continuum and those that might not be as informative are placed on the "Less" side.

   b. The team leader writes these on the master Evidence Wall Template.

3. The team leader then asks, "So if we want to answer the question, "How might we ensure that our collaborative team learning is evident to each of us on the team and to anyone that came into this space even if we weren't here? What can we learn from the kindergarten classroom where the products of learning are highly visible?"

   a. The team leader encourages the team to think of the following questions:

      i. What artifacts would be most informative to us as a team and others who come into our collaborative space? (The example Evidence Wall Template or a copy of the PLC 2.0 Toolkit can be used to give the team some ideas.)

      ii. Where would the artifacts be placed to have the highest impact?

      iii. When would the artifacts be collected, specifically in terms of the collaborative meeting dates?

PLC 2.0 Toolkit

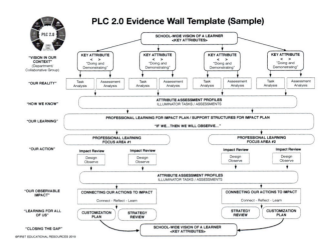

4. The team leader listens to the group and constructions draft "We will … statements" such as:
   a. "In order to make our learning observable for our team and those who come to our space, we will…
      i. ensure that each weekly meeting has a tangible product.
      ii. ensure that the product:
         1. can speak for itself.
         2. is of high quality.
         3. informs the team.
      iii. make that tangible product a visible artifact by placing it on our evidence wall.
      iv. periodically invite team members from other collaborative teams to our space to:
         1. share the products of their learning.
         2. ensure that the learning from each piece speaks for itself.
   b. NOTE: This is an example "We will …" statement. The team leader should construct a "We will …" statement that meets the goals of the team.
5. The team leader reads the statements to the group and asks for feedback on the statements. The statements should reflect the vision of an Evidence Wall and make their thinking observable to the team. These statements should then be recorded in the action portion of the Evidence Wall Template as the first artifact of team learning.

Part 5

Reflection (5 minutes)
1. The team reflects on how they might use the idea of context transfer in their classrooms with their students to inspire ideas or creative thinking.

Developing a Vision of a Learner - Multiple Perspectives

Part 1: What are the jobs of the future for our students? Try to think of both 'traditional' jobs (think doctor, engineer, tradesperson, etc.) and less traditional (artificial intelligence policy worker, 3D fashion designer, etc).

Part 2: Consider your list above. If you wanted to make your list more complete, what other perspectives could you gather from your school community? Beyond your school community? In higher education? In business or industry? List at 4-6 perspectives that could help you get a better picture of the work of the future.

Part 3: Pick three of the perspectives above, and place their titles in each of the boxes below. What are skills/attributes/characteristics that you believe they might want from our learners as they leave the K-12 system?

Perspective #1: _____
Desired attributes/skills from our students
• • • • • • •

Perspective #1: _____
Desired attributes/skills from our students
• • • • • • •

Perspective #1: _____
Desired attributes/skills from our students
• • • • • • •

Part 4: What are the common attributes from each of these perspectives? If you were to prioritize these common attributes, which ones would you see as most important for students to give them the best opportunities for success in the future?

Prioritized List of Attributes of a Learner
• • • • • • •

PLC 2.0 Toolkit

©FIRST EDUCATIONAL RESOURCES 2019

©FIRST EDUCATIONAL RESOURCES 2019

MAKING OUR ATTRIBUTES OF A LEARNER OBSERVABLE

Prioritized List of Attributes of a Learner

IN OUR STUDENTS

Part 5a: Select one of your attributes from above. If this attribute was being done well in your school, what would you observe students DOING and DEMONSTRATING in their classrooms. Be as specific as you can - what would you see and hear?

IN OUR EDUCATORS

Part 5b: If this attribute was being done well in your school, what would you observe teachers DOING and DEMONSTRATING in their classrooms. Be as specific as you can - what would you see and hear?

IN OUR TASKS AND ASSESSMENTS

Part 5c: If this attribute was being done well in your school, what are the TASKS you would observe that would require students to learn this skill? What would the tasks require students to DO and DEMONSTRATE. What ASSESSMENTS would you see to reflect this learning?

IN OUR STRUCTURES AND SUPPORTS

Part 5d: If this attribute was being done well in your school, what are the STRUCTURES AND SUPPORTS you would observe to enable this attribute to be taught and learned? Be specific.

17   *PLC 2.0 Toolkit*

Vision of a Learner Protocol (Part 1)

This tool helps school leaders, collaborative teams and partner groups to co-create the attributes that will begin to comprise The Vision of a Learner.

Prep Time: 5-10 mins

Time for Activity: 60-80 minutes

Use this protocol to have your collaborative team, staff and partner groups:
- consider the skills and competencies students will require for the future using multiple perspectives.
- to make the thinking of the group visible in order to come to consensus on the attributes that best serve students in their future.

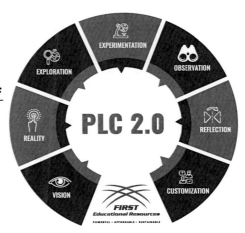

Things You Will Need:
- copies of the Developing a Vision of a Learning - Multiple Perspectives tool for each participant
- Post-it notes (lots), pens, markers
- large poster paper
- data projector, screen, laptop, sound

Part 1

Stepping Into The Future (15 minutes)
1. The team leader welcomes the group, and discusses the idea of how the only constant in our world is change, and that we are preparing students for jobs that have yet to be created and to solve problems that have yet to be discovered.
2. The team leader asks the group to think about the biggest change that they have seen in their lifetime, and what they think the biggest change will be in the future. The leader gives 3 minutes for partner chat then asks pairs to share out.
3. The team leader discusses how we have one set of perspectives on what the future holds, but reminds the group that it's always important to get multiple perspectives.
    a. This is difficult considering how busy we are!
4. This leads into the video, a short (under 10 minute) video on the future. The team

PLC 2.0 Toolkit 18

leader asks the group to use a "Three Struck Me" thinking routine, and consider three things that struck them about the video:

    a. TWO things that surprised them, and

    b. ONE thing that challenged their thinking.

5. Group shares out.

Part 2

Skills For The Future (10 minutes)

1. Participants are asked individually to fill out Part 1 of the Vision of a Learner Protocol that asks them to consider the jobs of the future for their students.

2. Once they have done this, participants are asked to stand and use the "Give One, Take One" thinking routine.

    a. Participants take their list, find a partner and "give" the other partner a job that the other partner doesn't have on their list.

    b. Once they give one, the partner "gets" a job that they don't have on their list.

    c. Repeat with 3 other people to grow their list of jobs of the future.

3. Participants return to their seats.

Part 3

Developing Different Perspectives (15 minutes)

1. Participants are asked to fill out Part 2 of the Vision of a Learner Protocol by considering other perspectives they might need to gather in order to develop a fulsome perspective of the skills needed for the future.

2. The team leader asks the groups to share some of the different perspectives to consider and helps to create three different personas, such as post-secondary (colleges, universities and trades), parents, and educators.

3. Individual participants are asked to brainstorm the desired attributes and skills people from each of these perspectives would like to see in students when they leave school.

    a. These are filled in each one of the Perspective boxes in Part 3 of the Vision of a Learner Protocol.

4. The groups are asked to take their three lists, look for commonalities among the three lists and create the Prioritized List of Attributes of a Learner at the bottom of the first page. The team leader asks participants to place each of these prioritized characteristics/attributes onto separate Post-It notes.

PLC 2.0 Toolkit

Part 4

Affinity Clustering for Common Attributes (15 minutes)

1. Participants stand with each of their Post-It notes and line up single file in front of a large whiteboard of flat-surface.
2. The first participant places their first Post-It note on the wall and goes to the back of the line.
3. The second participant approaches the wall:
   a. if there characteristic is similar (i.e. "punctual" and "time management"), they place their characteristic close to the first one.
   b. if there characteristic is different (i.e. "punctual" and "articulate"), they place it on a different spot on the wall.
4. The participants follow one-by-one, placing their Post-it notes either near other similar descriptors or in their own spots, forming "cluster clouds" until at Post-It notes are up.
5. The group looks at the different clusters and creates common overarching attributes that describe each cloud.
6. The goal is to get four to six common attributes that the group feels will provide the most opportunities for the students to be successful beyond their years at the school.

Part 5

Reflection (5 minutes)

1. The team leader asks the group to look at the co-designed list and consider which other groups could help further co-create a compelling vision for the entire community.
2. The list is posted on the Evidence Wall for the collaborative team.

PLC 2.0 Toolkit

Vision of a Learner Protocol (Part 2)

This tool helps school leaders, collaborative teams and partner groups to deconstruct the attributes to co-create an observable Vision of a Learner.

Prep time: 5-10 mins

Time for Activity: 60-80 minutes (NOTE: this could be done together with Part 1 if schools had a longer session or professional learning day)

Use this protocol to have your collaborative team, staff and partner groups:
- help make the attributes of a learner from Part 1 become observable through the lens of what students and teachers would be DOING and DEMONSTRATING.

Things You Will Need:
- the list of attributes from Vision of a Learner Protocol-Part 1, each in large font on Letter Size Paper (i.e. "CRITICAL THINKER", or "GLOBAL CITIZEN" etc...
- "Attribute Stations" - 3 large pieces of poster paper for each attribute:
    - 1 labelled "What would STUDENTS be doing and demonstrating?"
    - 1 labelled "What would EDUCATORS be doing and demonstrating?"
    - 1 labelled "What are the types of TASKS/ACTIVITIES that would allow students to demonstrate this attribute?"
- pens, markers
- groups of 3-4

Part 1

Making Our Vision Observable (45 minutes)
1. The team leader welcomes the group, and highlights the attributes that were developed in Vision of a Learner Protocol - Part 1.
    a. This would be the agreed upon list between all involved partner groups.
2. The team leader divides participants into groups of 3-4 and assigns each to an Attribute Station.

3. The team leader tells participants that they will have six minutes at their Attribute Station to brainstorm:
    a. what students would be doing and demonstrating, if they were observed performing this attribute at a high level of proficiency,
    b. what educators would be doing and demonstrating if they were observed teaching this attribute at a high level of proficiency, and
    c. what types of tasks would require students to demonstrate this attribute at a high level of proficiency.
    d. While teams are working, the leader should prompt participants to be specific with their observations (i.e. instead of "Questioning" participants should say "Asking non-procedural questions related to the concept being taught" or instead of "Facilitating" participants should say "Redirecting student questions to the class for the class to answer").
4. After six minutes, groups rotate clockwise to the next station to add to the thoughts of the previous group, and repeat at each station.
    a. The team leader may choose to shorten the times after the 3rd or 4th station switch, as the ideas may begin to repeat.

Part 2

Streamlining Our Thinking (10 minutes)
1. Participants return to their first station and begin to synthesize the results, looking for similarities on each of the poster charts for students, educators and tasks. (3 minutes)
2. The team leader asks each group to consider each of the points from the student, educator and task brainstorms and asks the question, "How would we actually observe this?" to ensure that each piece would be readily observable in classrooms.
    a. If not, the groups try to "uptick" the point to make it more observable.
3. Once they have done this, participants are asked to pick the top four in each category (four for students, four for educators, and four for tasks) that they felt best represented what would be observed in a classroom when the attribute was being demonstrated at a high level.
4. Participants circle each of the four—these are their "prime examples."
5. Participants return to their seats.

Part 3

Honing in on Observables (15 minutes)
1. Each participant is given a marker. Participants are asked to do a 2-3 minute gallery walk to examine each of the different attributes and the "Doing and Demonstrating"

PLC 2.0 Toolkit   22

charts that people have created.

2. Participants are then asked to use their marker and vote for the two descriptors on each Doing and Demonstrating chart paper that they feel are most observable and indicative of the attribute.

   a. (Example: for the attribute "critical thinker," each participant would star two Doing and Demonstrating descriptors on the student chart paper, the educator chart paper and task chart paper.)

3. The result will be a list of the observables for each of the attribute areas.

Part 4

Reflection (7 minutes)

1. The team leader asks the group to gallery walk the room to see what people have prioritized and asks the group to reflect on two things:

   a. Is there anything missing?

   b. How does research support what we are saying?

2. The team leader opens discussion up and adds notes to chart paper as the group discusses their reflections.

3. Artifacts from this process are placed on the Evidence Wall for the collaborative team.

Vision To Outcomes Connector Tool

In PLC 2.0, developing our Vision of a Learner can sometimes be a challenge with our busy, demanding and full curricula. Therefore it's important for us to be able to look at our existing outcomes in order to ensure we prioritize the ones which most closely align to the attributes from our Vision. Use this tool to being the process of connecting your curricular outcomes in your area to your departmental or school vision so that you can 'double dip' to teach AND those that get us closer to our vision at the same time.

Department/Collaborative Team: _____   **Date:** _____

Grade Level/Grouping and Subject (IE. Grade 4 Science)

Enter Your Attribute Here:

IN OUR STUDENTS: If this attribute was being done well in your school, what would you observe students DOING and DEMONSTRATING in their classrooms. Be as specific as you can - what would you see and hear?

IN OUR TASK DESIGN: What are the types of tasks that would require students to DO and DEMONSTRATE this attribute? How would they be designed? What might the products look like? What would be the style and types of questions that might be used?

ATTRIBUTE SCAN: Look through your learning standards/curriculum documents. Which standards connect to what we want to observe in our students and our tasks, as outlined above? Write the standards that best connect below.

PLC 2.0 Toolkit

©FIRST EDUCATIONAL RESOURCES 2019

24

Opinion Line - Prioritizing Our Learning Standards to Align with Our Vision

Consider the outcomes as a results of your Attribute Scan on the previous page. As an individual, place the outcomes along the continuum considering how critical that outcome is to the success of your students AND how connected that outcome is to the attribute you are focusing on. Then, once each member of your collaborative team has finished this individually, be prepared to share as a group and negotiate where the outcome would lie in terms of priority.

"Higher Priority Outcomes"

Highly connected to our Vision AND critical to success in this subject area

"Lower Priority Outcomes"

Less connected to our Vision and less critical to success in this subject area

Reflection Question: How can this guide the design of our units and our lessons? How can we ensure the higher priority outcomes are actually given a higher priority in our instruction?

©FIRST EDUCATIONAL RESOURCES 2019

PLC 2.0 Toolkit

Vision To Outcomes Connector Tool

This tool helps departments and grade level groupings connect their curriculum to their Vision of a Learner.

Prep time: 5-10 mins to gather materials

Time for Activity: 45 mins

Use this protocol to have your collaborative team:
- examine their curriculum outcomes of an upcoming unit/set of units through the lens of an attribute that comprises the school vision Vision of a Learner.
- find "high-priority outcomes" (outcomes that are highly connected to our Vision and critical to the success of students) to focus the team's time and efforts on improving our practice in these areas.

Things You Will Need:
- copies of the 'Vision to Outcomes Connector Tool' for each participant
- copies (electronic or paper) of curriculum documents that are relevant to upcoming lessons for the group
- Post-It notes, markers
- two letter sized pieces of paper, one labelled "Higher Priority Outcomes" and the second labelled "Lower Priority Outcomes"

Part 1

Re-visiting the Vision (5 minutes)
1. Team leader has the group fill in the top of the protocol, including the attribute that the group is going to focus on for the collaborative meeting (i.e. critical thinking, global citizenship, etc).
2. Team leader starts by saying, "This afternoon during our meeting, we are going to be planning for our upcoming unit on <unit name>. What we will do is look through our curriculum documents to see if we can find those outcomes that are both vital to learn AND will allow us to observe our students demonstrating <student attribute> at the

same time. We call these high-priority outcomes. But before we do this, we need to ensure that we are looking at our outcomes through the lens the attribute that we are going to be focusing on."

3. The team leader asks team to recall the Vision of a Learner and to describe what they observe students DOING and DEMONSTRATING if they were demonstrating this attribute with a high level of proficiency in this area.

   a. The team leader asks the question, "What would we observe our students doing and demonstrating when they were doing this well?"

   b. The group brainstorms ideas, making sure they are being specific and descriptive with their observations. The group is encouraged to ask, "What would we actually see and hear if students were doing that?"

4. The team leader repeats the process, but this time talks about task design. The team leader asks the group, "What are the types of tasks that would require students to do and demonstrate the skill or attribute?"

   a. The group brainstorms and records the specific activities that they would want to observe in the classrooms that would give the best opportunity to see students demonstrating that attribute.

Part 2

Curriculum Scan (15 minutes)

1. The team then begins to look through the curriculum documents and highlight those outcomes that they feel give the best opportunity for them to observe their students demonstrating the attribute. The team leader suggests to the group that they try and find five to seven of those outcomes each.

2. The team records those outcomes onto individual Post-it notes .

3. The team then takes their Post-it notes to a wall or flat surface and begins to place them up on the wall one by one in Affinity Cluster (see Vision of a Learner Protocol (Part 1)).

4. The team looks at the Affinity Clusters to find common outcomes suggested by group members. At this point, the group removes duplicates.

Part 3

Opinion Line Prioritizing (20 minutes)

1. On an adjacent wall, the team leader places the two signs that are on letter-sized paper. They place the Lower Priority Outcomes sign on the left portion of the wall and they place the Higher Priority Outcomes sign on the right portion of the wall.

2. One by one the group places the outcomes from the Post-it notes on the priority

continuum. The team leader reminds the group that there can be no ties, that if one outcome is closed in terms of priority to another, the group has to pick and come to consensus on which outcome is a higher priority.

    a. The team leader emphasizes that by putting something lower on the priority scale does not mean that it will not be covered, but rather that we will spend more time covering the higher priority outcomes that are both highly connected to our vision and critical to success in the subject.

3. The result is a prioritized list of outcomes for the upcoming unit that can guide the design of the tasks and activities that will allow students to learn the outcome at a high level and demonstrate the outcome in an observable fashion.

4. This list is added to the Evidence Wall for the group.

Part 4

Reflect (5 minutes)

1. At the conclusion, the team leader asks the group to reflect upon what they've learned and how this will guide their task design based on what they want students to do and demonstrate.

Vision-To-Collaborative Team Connector Tool

OUR SCHOOL VISION OF A LEARNER:

DEPARTMENT/COLLABORATIVE TEAM:

VISION OF A LEARNER ATTRIBUTE:

IN OUR STUDENTS: When our students are proficient at this attribute in our area, you will see our students DOING and DEMONSTRATING:

-
-
-
-
-
-

IN OUR TEACHING: In order to develop this attribute in our area, you will observe us DOING and DEMONSTRATING

-
-
-
-
-
-

IN OUR ACTIVITIES AND ASSESSMENTS: In order for us to observe this attribute being done in our area, you will see our students doing tasks such as:

©FIRST EDUCATIONAL RESOURCES 2019

PLC 2.0 Toolkit

Vision-To-Collaborative Team Connector Tool

This tool helps departments and grade level groupings develop a departmental-specific vision based on the School Vision of a Learner.

Prep time: 5-10 mins to gather materials

Time for Activity: 45 mins

Use this protocol to have your collaborative team:
- examine their content area/grade level grouping through the lens of an attribute that comprises the school Vision of a Learner.
- articulate a descriptive and visible set of characteristics/features that would be demonstrated by students, educators and activities for a specific attribute that an observer would see in a classroom in the team content or grade level area (i.e. critical thinking in intermediate science).

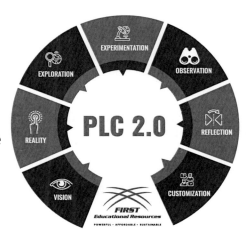

Things You Will Need:
- copies of the Vision-to-Collaborative Team Connector Tool for each participant
- Post-It notes, markers
- 3 stations with large pieces of chart paper
    - one labeled "In our Students"
    - one labeled "In our Teaching"
    - one labeled "In Activities and Assessments"
- OPTIONAL: short article/reading on the attribute that the team is working on

Part 1

Setting The Stage (2 minutes)
1. Team leader has the group fill in the top of the Vision-to-Collaborative Team Connector Tool, including the school Vision of a Learner and attribute that the group is focusing on (i.e. critical thinking, global citizenship, etc).
2. Team leader starts by saying "This afternoon during our meeting, we are going to begin the process of grounding the School Vision of a Learner into our work in our

PLC 2.0 Toolkit

classrooms. While having an overarching vision for our students is vital for our school, we also want our team to <u>own</u> this attribute in our team make sure that our students have a clear picture of what that looks like in our area."

    a. Team leader highlights that things like critical thinking can't be taught independently of content - "When we ask someone to think critically, it needs to be in a content area. We can't just say "We want you to be a critical thinker!", we want our students to be a critical thinker in our area."

3. OPTIONAL: article reading in attribute area (i.e. article on 'critical thinking in history' or 'communication in the world of science').

Part 2

Brainstorming the Departmental/Grade Group Vision (18 minutes)

1. The team leader divides the collaborative team into smaller groups (pairs or threes), and assigns each team to one of the pieces of poster paper (students, teaching, or activities and assessments).
2. The team leader tells participants that they will have 5 minutes at their station to brainstorm:
   a. what students would be doing and demonstrating, if they were observed performing this attribute at a high level of proficiency,
   b. what educators would be doing and demonstrating if they were observed teaching this attribute at a high level of proficiency, and
   c. what types of activities/assessments would best require students to demonstrate this attribute at a high level of proficiency.
   d. The attribute asks participants to be specific in their observations:
      i. From "Questioning" to "Asking non-procedural questions related to the concept being taught."
      ii. From "Facilitating" to "Re-directing student questions to the class for the class to answer."
3. After 5 minutes, groups rotate clockwise to the next station to add to the thoughts of the previous group, and repeat at each station.

Part 3

Streamlining Our Thinking (10 minutes)

1. Participants return to their first station and begin to synthesize the results, looking for similarities on each of the poster charts for students, educators and activities/ assessments. (3 minutes)
2. The team leader asks each group to consider each of the points from the student,

educator and task brainstorms and asks the question "How would we actually observe this in our department?" to ensure that each piece would be readily observable in classrooms.

    a. If not, the groups try to "uptick" the point to make it more observable.

3. Once they have done this, team members at each station are asked to pick the top four in each category (4 for students, 4 for educators, and 4 for tasks) that they felt best represented what would be observed in a classroom when the attribute was being demonstrated at a high level.

    a. Team members use a marker to circle each of the 4--these are their 'prime examples.'

4. Team members return to their seats.

Part 4

Coming to Consensus on Observables (5 minutes)

1. Each participant is given a marker. Participants are asked to do a 2-3 minute gallery walk to examine each of the different attributes and the 'doing and demonstrating' charts that people have created.

2. Participants are then asked to use their marker and 'vote' for the two descriptors on each 'doing and demonstrating' chart paper that they feel are most observable and indicative of the attribute.

    a. (Example: for the attribute 'critical thinker' each participant would star two 'doing and demonstrating' descriptors on the student chart paper, the educator chart paper and task chart paper)

3. The result will be a list of the observables for each of 'students', 'teachers' and 'activities and assessments' that comprise the departmental vision of a learner.

Part 5

Reflection (7 minutes)

1. The team leader asks the group to gallery walk the room to see what people have prioritized, and are asked to reflect on two things.

    a. Is there anything missing?

    b. How does research support what we are saying?

2. The team leader opens discussion up and adds notes to chart paper.

3. The final chart paper is added to the Evidence Wall for the group.

PLC 2.0 Toolkit

Vision To Task 'Feed Forward' Tool

In PLC 2.0, it is vital for us to look at the activities and tasks that we do in our units and lessons and examine them through the lens of what they ask students to DO and to DEMONSTRATE. Use this tool to examine activity sequences or approaches that could be taken to a high priority outcome through the lens of our attributes and get 'feed-forward' to move it even closer to the learning that we want in our classrooms.

Department/Collaborative Team: _____   Grade Level/Grouping/Subject (IE. Grade 6 math): _____

OUR ATTRIBUTE/FOCUS: _____

DEVELOPING OUR ATTRIBUTE LENS

ANALYZING OUR TASK SEQUENCE THROUGH THE ATTRIBUTE LENS

STEP 1: VISION - What would students be DOING and DEMONSTRATING if they were highly proficient in this attribute focus area (List these below - be specific)

STEP 2: CLARIFY - Outline the planned activity sequence below. What will students be doing and demonstrating? What will be the products of learning?

STEP 3: FEED FORWARD- Where could we go with this activity sequence to allow us to observe even more of the characteristics from the vision from Step 1 in our students?

Step 4: CONSOLIDATE - What are the next steps? How can we support?

LEARN: What can we learn from this feed-forward process that we can apply to our future collaboration together and our future learning?

©FIRST EDUCATIONAL RESOURCES 2019

33

PLC 2.0 Toolkit

Vision To Task 'Feed-Forward' Tool

This tool helps collaborative teams give "feed-forward" to each other to connect their tasks and activities to their Vision of a Learner.

Prep time: 2 mins to photocopy protocol

Time for Activity: 15 mins per task/activity sequence

Use this protocol to have your collaborative team:

- examine their tasks through the lens of an attribute that comprises the school Vision of a Learner.

Things You Will Need:

- copies of the 'Vision to Task Feed-Forward' Tool for each participant
- timer
- tasks or activities in an upcoming unit from the department
- OPTIONAL: short article/reading on the attribute that the team is working on

---

Part 1

Setting The Stage (2 minutes)

1. Team leader starts by saying, "This afternoon during our meeting, we are going to be grounding the school Vision of a Learner into our tasks and activities in our classrooms. Sometimes we want our students to demonstrate things like creative thinking in our area, but we might need some help to provide the creative license to do so. That is what we are here for as a collaborative group."
2. Team leader provides some guidelines for "<u>feed-forward</u>," the feedback that we give to our peers when we want to help propel them and their work forward.
   a. Groups should establish their feed-forward. Some examples are:
      i. Start with the best of intentions
      ii. Critique the content, not the person
      iii. 'Qu-answers' are not permitted (questions that have an answer built into them; advice in disguise)
      iv. "Share the air" and listen rather than wait to speak

PLC 2.0 Toolkit   34

Part 2

Setting The Vision (3 minutes)

1. The team leader asks the group to consider the attribute in question (i.e. creative thinking) and says, "In our department/grade level, what would we observe students doing and demonstrating if they were at a high level of proficiency in this area?" (3 minutes)

   a. The group brainstorms (and refers to the departmental vision, if developed).

   b. The team leader jots down the ideas from the group, encouraging them to be specific and to avoid jargon ("What would someone who has never been to one of our classes see? How would they know?").

   c. Each of the group members jots these features down in the greyed out column (Step 1 on tool sheet).

2. Once the team has a shared understanding of the Attribute Lens, the team leader asks for a volunteer to put forward an activity that they have planned for the upcoming unit so the team can assess the task and give them feed-forward on it.

   a. Team leader reminds the group, "A strengths-based approach is vital, team! We are here to support and help make things better as a group."

Part 3

The Feed-Forward Protocol (Timed Protocol - 15 minutes sharp)

1. <u>Activity/Task Presentation:</u> (3 minutes) A team member is picked as the presenter. The presenter shares a task for the team to look at and gets three minutes to describe what the activity or task sequence will be, what students will be doing and demonstrating, and the observable products of learning. The presenter ends their three minutes with a question framed as, "What I am hoping the team can help me with is ..."

2. <u>Clarification:</u> (2 minutes) Collaborative team asks questions to clarify what has been presented (NO qu-answers)—things about the products, tasks, student groupings, assessments, etc.

3. <u>Feed-Forward:</u> (4 minutes) The collaborative team looks at the Vision column and uses this to give "warms" (positive feedback) and "wonders" (challenges or questions) about what has been presented. The presenter remains silent and takes notes under the Step 3 column. The presenter may choose to sit back from the group, so they are not tempted to respond (and they are not allowed to at this point).

4. <u>Consolidate:</u> (4 minutes) Presenter is given two minutes to surface their thinking from the Feed-Forward phase and starts with, "I appreciated the group saying..." The last two minutes are spent consolidating ideas, with the rest of the collaborative team helping the presenter think of next steps and how they can support the presenter.

35   *PLC 2.0 Toolkit*

5. <u>Learn:</u> (2 minutes) The group talks about the Feed-Forward process and discusses how they might be able to apply what they learned from the presenter in their own practice.

6. A copy of the Vision To Task "Feed Forward" Tool is attached to the collaborative team Evidence Wall.

NOTE: The Feed Forward Protocol can be repeated multiple times, depending on the length of collaborative team time available.

Illuminator Task/Assessment Idea Generator

In each of our areas, we have certain 'high priority outcomes' - outcomes that are highly connected to our Vision of a Learner, and important for the success of our students in our area or grade level. But which assessments let us observe what students DO and DEMONSTRATE in these outcome areas? Use this tool to generate ideas for these "ILLUMINATOR" tasks/assessments.

Department/Collaborative Team: _____

Grade Level/Grouping/Subject (IE. Grade 4 Science): _____

OUR ATTRIBUTE/FOCUS: _____

CREATIVE INSPIRATION PHRASES: "A task or assessment that covers <SECTION A> where students are doing and demonstrating <SECTION B> could look like...<BRAINSTORM>

SECTION A:

HIGH PRIORITY OUTCOME(S)—Upcoming Outcome(s) where students could DO and DEMONSTRATE this attribute (list below)

-
-
-
-
-
-
-

SECTION B:

What would we observe students DOING and DEMONSTRATING if they were at a high level of proficiency in this attribute or focus area?
Be specific.

-
-
-
-
-
-
-

BRAINSTORM:

What are the possible tasks/assessments you can generate when you combine Section A and Section B?

NEXT STEPS: From our Brainstorm, what do we already have that is similar? What might we need to create? Which ILLUMINATOR activities and assessments will we use to observe our students demonstrating these important outcomes AND our attribute/focus area?

©FIRST EDUCATIONAL RESOURCES 2019

PLC 2.0 Toolkit

Illuminator Task/Assessment Idea Generator

Use this tool to spark creative ideas and generate tasks and assessments that allow us to observe students DOING and DEMONSTRATING high-priority outcomes through the lens of our Vision of a Learner.

Prep Time: 5 mins to gather materials

Time for Activity: 25-40 mins

Use this protocol to have your collaborative team:
- to find/plan for opportunities in upcoming units to observe students demonstrating attributes from the Vision of a Learner AND complete high-priority content outcomes.
- leave with ideas and next steps for "illuminator" activities and assessments.
- to have fun and get creative juices flowing.

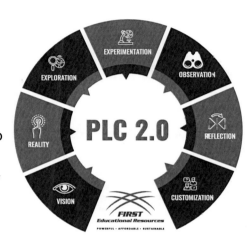

Things You Will Need:
- copies of the Illuminator Task/Assessment Idea Generator for each team member
- Post-it notes, chart paper and markers
- A list of high-priority outcomes from an upcoming unit from the Vision to Outcomes Connector Tool
    - NOTE: if high priority outcomes for the upcoming unit have yet to be determined, it is important for the group to do so
        - Take 15 minutes and use the Vision to Outcomes Connector Tool to generate a list of high priority outcomes
- Supporting curriculum documents for the upcoming unit as needed

Part 1

Setting the Focus (5-7 minutes)
1. The team leader hands out the Illuminator Task/Assessment Idea Generator for each team member, clarifies which upcoming unit is going to be discussed and picks a Vision of a Learner attribute.

PLC 2.0 Toolkit

a. Example: *Unit - Social Studies 9: Economics. Vision of a Learner Attribute: Effective, real world communicator*

2. The team leader asks the group to consider the focus attribute and what students would be doing and demonstrating for that attribute in the department/grade level and school level if they were proficient in the attribute.

   a. Think-Pair-All: team members write down what students would be doing and demonstrating on Post-It notes. When finished, they partner up and share. Finally, the team leader facilitates a whole group share so that everyone has a common understanding of the attribute.

   b. Team inputs from Think-Pair-All are placed into Section B of the tool.

Part 2

Creating Inspiration Phrases (15 minutes)

1. The team leader asks the group for the high-priority outcomes in the upcoming unit of study. The team recounts the high-priority outcomes, and why they are the ones that are most important for students to demonstrate.

   a. These are placed in Section A of the tool.

2. The team leader then splits the group into smaller groups of 2-3 members and asks them to generate Inspiration Phrases that combine the outcomes in Section A with the characteristics from Section B in the form of...

   a. "A task or assessment that covers <SECTION A> where students are doing and demonstrating <SECTION B> could look like ... <BRAINSTORM>

   b. For example, "A task that covers *<the role of competition in product markets, and its relationship to price and quality of goods and services>* where students are doing and demonstrating *<characteristics of effective, real-world communication>* could look like...

3. The team leader encourages the team to create Inspiration Phrases that lead to multiple possibilities and ideas. Each team writes their phrases on chart paper.

4. After 3-4 minutes, the team leader encourages the team to dig deeper, and even to "go wild" with their thinking, injecting wildcard ideas such as, "How could our questions change if we added another element..."

   a. "A task that covers *<the role of competition in product markets, and its relationship to price and quality of goods and services>* where students are doing and demonstrating *<characteristics of effective, real-world communication>* AND WERE

      i.   performing this for a live audience.

      ii. using social media.

      iii. creating something to teach students.

        iv.   utilizing infographics.

5. The resulting inspiration phrases are placed on the chart paper for the team to see.

Part 3

Brainstorming (15 minutes)

1. Team leader then asks the small groups to pick 2-3 inspiration phrases to generate ideas for Illuminator Tasks - tasks that "double dip" in terms of having students demonstrate the attribute and the high priority outcome in a way that the teacher can observe both at the same time.
2. The team leader encourages quantity first in terms of ideas, so that the team doesn't get bogged down in the details.
3. At the 10-minute mark, small groups share out their top ideas to the rest of the group.

Part 4

Next Steps (5 minutes)

1. Team leader asks the group, "Of our ideas, what do we already have that is similar? What might we need to create?"
2. Which Illuminator Activities and assessments will we use to observe our students demonstrating these important outcomes AND our attribute/focus area?
   a. Team leader has team fill out their own individual sheets and fills out the sheet with next steps and responsibilities in order to generate the activities and assessments for the future unit.
3. Team leader fills out a master copy, which goes on the Evidence Wall for the team.

PLC 2.0 Toolkit

Balanced Assessment Profile Tool

Department/Collaborative Team: _____   Grade Level/Grouping/Subject (IE. Grade 6 math): _____

ATTRIBUTE LENS

From our Vision of a Learner, our attribute focus is: _____

What would we observe students DOING and DEMONSTRATING if they were at a high level of proficiency in this attribute? Be specific.

• • • •

CREATING A BALANCED ASSESSMENT PROFILE

3 'types' of activities/assessments that allow us to observe our students DOING and DEMONSTRATING this attribute

A.
B.
C.

UPCOMING 'TYPE A' ACTIVITIES/ASSESSMENTS

A1.
A2.
A3.
A4.

UPCOMING 'TYPE B' ACTIVITIES/ASSESSMENTS

B1.
B2.
B3.
B4.

UPCOMING 'TYPE C' ACTIVITIES/ASSESSMENTS

C1.
C2.
C3.
C4.

TIMELINE: Approximate the timeline of the activities/assessments for this attribute by writing them (ie. 'B3') on the timeline below.

BEGINNING OF TERM → MIDTERM → END OF TERM →

LEARN: What have we learned about our assessment of this attribute? What do we need to continue doing? What might we need to change? What are our next steps?

©FIRST EDUCATIONAL RESOURCES 2019

PLC 2.0 Toolkit

Balanced Assessment Profile Tool

This tool helps collaborative teams create a balanced assessment plan through the lens of an attribute from the Vision of A Learner.

Prep Time: 5 mins to photocopy protocol and find chart paper, markers and Post-Its

Time for Activity: 50 minutes

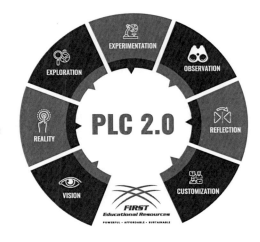

Use this protocol to have your collaborative team:
- look an upcoming unit, term or semester through the lens of an attribute (i.e. critical thinking) and develop an assessment profile to gain an understanding of:
    - the types of activities and assessments being used.
    - the timing of the tasks and activities.
    - the balance of assessment types.
- to examine whether our current attribute assessment profile allows us to observe our students demonstrating this attribute at a high level of proficiency, or if there are adjustments that we can make to accurately observe our students' abilities in this attribute area.

Things You Will Need:
- copies of the Balanced Assessment Profile Tool for each participant
- general outline of tasks and activities for an upcoming term for the collaborative group
- Post-It notes, markers, three pieces of chart paper, and three small signs
    - One piece of chart paper with "Type A," one with "Type B" and one with "Type C"
    - One sign with "Beginning of Term," one with "Midterm" and one with "End of Term"
- OPTIONAL: copy of the departmental and/or school Vision of a Learner

PLC 2.0 Toolkit

Part 1

Setting The Stage (5 minutes)

1. Team leader starts by saying, "This afternoon during our meeting, we are going to be creating an assessment profile of one of the attributes from our department/ school Vision of a Learner. The goal of today's meeting is for our collaborative team to determine the types of activities and assessments that best allow us to observe <learner attribute>, and then to look at our own activities and assessments, when we do those things, and determine if we have a balance of assessment types for each of our learners to demonstrate <learner attribute>."

2. The team leader asks the group to consider the attribute in question (i.e. real world communication') and says, "In our department/grade grouping, what would we observe students doing and demonstrating if they were at a high level of proficiency in this area?" (3 minutes)

    a. The group brainstorms (and refers to the departmental version of the Vision of a Learner-if developed).

    b. Team leader jots down the ideas from the group, encouraging them to be specific and to avoid jargon ("What would someone who has never been to one of our classes see? How would they know?").

    c. Each member jots down these features in the Attribute Lens box.

Part 2

Examining our Current Activities and Assessments (20 minutes)

1. The team leader asks the collaborative group to switch gears and consider the attribute lens from a different perspective.

    a. "If this is what we would want to see students doing and demonstrating in this attribute area, what are the <u>types</u> of activities and assessments that allow us to observe each of our learners demonstrating this attribute at a high level of proficiency?"

    b. The team leader asks the group to write 4-6 activities and assessments that they currently do in their classes that allow them to observe their students demonstrating different characteristics from the attribute lens (i.e. real world communication). (3 minutes)

        i. These are written separately on Post-It notes and placed up on a flat surface in the collaborative area.

        ii. Duplicates are placed on top of each other.

2. The team leader then asks the group to examine all the activities on the Post-it notes and to group similar type activities into broader categories.

a. Examples include "writing tasks for an authentic audience," "creating multimedia documents" or "oral presentations."
3. Once the categories have been determined, the team leader asks the group to pick the <u>top three types</u> of activities and assessments that,
    a. allow for the best opportunities for us to observe the attribute, and
    b. provide a balanced assessment profile where students are able to demonstrate the attribute in different ways.
4. These top three types are listed as Type A, Type B and Type C in the center box on the Balanced Assessment Profile Tool and on the large pieces of chart paper.

Part 3

Checking for Balance (15 minutes)
1. The group then categorizes each Post-It note with an A, B or C and places them onto the appropriate chart paper that fits the activity or assessment best.
    a. The team leader records their grouping on the Balanced Assessment Profile Tool.
2. The team leader asks each team member to reflect on what they noticed about the activities and assessments for their learners.
    a. "What are we noticing about our activities and assessments in this attribute area? Do we have a balanced assessment profile that allows us to effectively observe our students doing and demonstrating <real world communication>?"
    b. The group discusses what they are noticing, what they are doing well with assessing this attribute, and what they might need to change to create a balanced approach to assess this attribute.
3. The team leader then takes the three signs and makes a Term Time Continuum by spreading them out across a flat surface from "Beginning of Term," "Midterm" and "End of Term."
    a. The team transfers their Post-It notes from the Type Charts to the Term Time Continuum.
    b. Team leader records their responses on their Balanced Assessment Profile Tool.
4. The team leader asks each team member to reflect on what they notice about the tasks for their learners.
    a. "What are we noticing about our activities and assessments from a time perspective? Do we have a balanced assessment profile that allows us to effectively observe our students progressing in this attribute area <real world communication> over time? What are we doing well? What might we need to change?"
    b. The group discusses what they are noticing in terms of the timing of activities and assessments of this attribute.

PLC 2.0 Toolkit

Part 4

Learn (5 minutes)

1. The team leader asks for the group to reflect on the activity.
    a. "What have we learned about our assessment of this attribute? What do we need to continue doing? What might we need to change? What are our next steps?"
    b. The group discusses how they can best observe all of their learners doing and demonstrating this attribute at a high level of proficiency.
2. The team leader's "master" Balanced Assessment Profile Tool goes on the Evidence Wall for the collaborative team.

Activity/Assessment Analysis Tool

In each of our areas, we assess certain 'high priority outcomes' - outcomes that are highly connected to our Vision of a Learner AND important for the success of our students in our area or grade level. But does the style and format of our assessments allow our students to demonstrate these attributes? Use this tool to determine your current assessment profile and future work that will allow your team to have a complete assessment picture of one of your areas of focus in your Vision of a Learner.

Department/Collaborative Team: _____   **Grade Level/Grouping/Subject (IE. Grade 6 math):** _____

Our Attribute/Focus: _____

High Priority Outcomes—Outcome(s) where we can observe students DOING and DEMONSTRATING this attribute

ANALYZING OUR CURRENT ASSESSMENT PROFILE FOR THIS ATTRIBUTE/AREA OF FOCUS

STEP 1: What would students be DOING and DEMONSTRATING if they were highly proficient in this attribute focus area (List 5 below - be specific)	**STEP 2:** What are the tasks/assessments we currently do that allow us to observe students demonstrating this characteristic	**STEP 3:** Where we need to go: tasks/assessments we might need to create to allow us to observe this characteristic	**Step 4:** Our Next Step

PLC 2.0 Toolkit

©FIRST EDUCATIONAL RESOURCES 2019

46

Activity/Assessment Analysis Tool

Use this tool to help the team determine how the activities/assessments in an upcoming unit can be adapted to help us observe our students demonstrating our Vision of a Learner.

Prep Time: 5 minutes to
- photocopy Activity/Assessment Analysis Tool for each team member
- gather curriculum documents and/or unit plans for an upcoming unit
- get Post-It notes and markers

Time for Activity: 50 mins

Use this protocol to have your collaborative team:
- analyze the activities and assessments in an upcoming unit through the lens of a Vision of a Learner.
- determine next steps needed to adapt outcomes and activities in order to give more opportunities to observe students demonstrating the Vision of a Learner.

Things You Will Need:
- a copy of the Activity/Assessment Analysis Tool for each team member
- unit plans or curriculum documents from an upcoming unit for the team from
- a list of existing activities and assessments normally observed in the unit
- Post-It notes and markers

Part 1

Setting the Focus (10 minutes)
1. The team leader begins by welcoming the group and setting the stage for the discussion:
    a. "The purpose of today's meeting is for us to look at the activities and assessments of the upcoming unit to:
        i. determine how we currently observe student learning around our Vision of a Learner and,

  ii. decide which methods should be adapted to make the attributes of our Vision of a Learner more observable."

2. The team decides which of the attributes from their Vision of a Learner is going to be the focus for the collaborative meeting (i.e. effective communication skills in junior Social Studies).

3. The team leader asks the team to pull out their unit plans and curriculum documents for the upcoming unit and says,

  a. "As a team, we are going to be looking for the high-priority outcomes (outcomes critical for us to observe and our students to demonstrate their understanding of the focus attribute)." An example would be effective communication skills in junior Social Studies.

  b. The team looks for multiple outcomes that lend themselves to demonstrating the attribute.

    i. The team leader emphasizes that every outcome cannot be essential, nor does every outcome necessarily lend itself to the focus attribute.

Part 2

Doing and Demonstrating - Recognizing the Attribute (10 minutes)

1. Once the high-priority outcomes have been determined, the team leader asks the group to shift their focus to the attribute:

  a. "If our students in junior Social Studies were demonstrating this attribute at a high level of proficiency <i.e. effective communication skills>, what would we observe them doing and demonstrating? Write five specific look-fors that we would see on individual Post-It notes."

    i. The group writes their five descriptors.

    ii. Examples include:

      1. "able to adapt their communication to suit different audiences"

      2. "able to communicate a message using multiple forms of media"

2. The group uses the Affinity Cluster protocol (see Vision of a Learner Protocol (Part 1)) to gain consensus on what they would observe.

  a. Lining up single file, one by one, participants place their Post-It notes on a wall or flat surface.

  b. If the Post-It notes are the same or similar to others that are up on the wall, the next in line places theirs below the similar ones.

  c. If the Post-It note is different, it is placed in a different spot on the flat surface to form a new affinity cluster.

    i. Example: "adapt their communication to suit different audiences" and "using different forms of media to communicate" might be put in a

PLC 2.0 Toolkit 48

similar cluster, but "provide a compelling argument" might be put in a different spot to form a new cluster.

3. The team looks at the Affinity Clusters and comes to consensus on five observables that they would see in their students if they were doing and demonstrating this attribute at a high level of proficiency.

    a. These are written in the Step 1 column on the tool.

Part 3

Examining our current practice (5 minutes)

1. The team leader asks the group to consider the activities and assessments they currently use to determine students' knowledge of these high-priority outcomes.

    a. "What are the activities and assessments that we currently do in our classes where students can demonstrate each of the characteristics of our attribute <i.e. effective communication in Junior Social Studies> in the Step 1 column?"

    b. The group lists their current activities/assessments in the Step 2 column next to the characteristic in the Step 1 that the activity or assessment best exemplifies. Activities and assessments can go next to multiple characteristics if they fit into more than one spot.

Part 4

Determining Design Adjustments (15 minutes)

1. The team leader then asks the group, "With each of these activities and assessments, what are the modifications that we might need to do in order to give our students more opportunity to demonstrate this attribute <effective communication> using this outcome?"

    a. For example, the group might decide to adjust an activity so it requires students to communicate a message in three different ways rather than just one to determine if students are "able to communicate a message using multiple forms of media."

2. The group repeats this process for the other activities and assessments listed to ensure they provide the best opportunities for the team to double dip by observing the outcome and the attribute.

3. After making tweaks to current activities and assessments, the team leader asks, "Are there any aspects of this attribute that we are not able to observe in our students? Are there activities that we might need to add?"

    a. The group determines any gaps and makes suggestions for activities/ assessments that might help them address any items in the Step 1 column.

Part 5

Next Steps (10 minutes)

1. The team looks at all of the suggestions that are written in Step 3, and the team leader says, "We have a number of ideas on how we can alter some of the work that we are doing to this point and a couple of things that we might need to add—how should we prioritize these for the upcoming unit? Who can take the lead?

2. The team looks at the suggestions through two lenses—potential impact and ease of implementation

    a. The team leader asks the team to look at each box in the Step 4 (Our Next Step column) and to score each next step with two numbers:

        i. A rating of 1-5 for potential impact to demonstrate attribute (5 being highest impact).

        ii. A rating of 1-5 for ease of implementation (5 being easiest to implement).

        iii. Each team member's total score (out of 10) for that next step is tallied.

            1. For example, a team member rates a step as 4 out of 5 for potential impact and 3 out of 5 for ease of implementation= 8/10.

        iv. The team can use this scoring system to help prioritize next steps.

3. The team assigns any to-do's to team members and notes a time for when the team will check in to report back on progress and needed support.

4. The "master" Activity/Assessment Analysis Tool is placed on the team Evidence Wall by the team leader.

PLC 2.0 Toolkit

Professional Learning for Observable Impact Tool

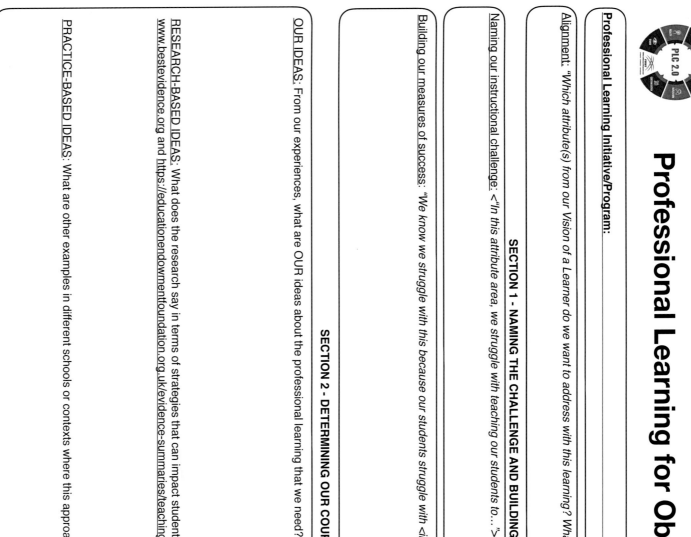

Professional Learning Initiative/Program: _____ **Date:** _____

Alignment: *"Which attribute(s) from our Vision of a Learner do we want to address with this learning? What elements of this attribute?"*

SECTION 1 - NAMING THE CHALLENGE AND BUILDING OUR MEASURES OF SUCCESS

Naming our instructional challenge: <*"In this attribute area, we struggle with teaching our students to…"*>

Building our measures of success: *"We know we struggle with this because our students struggle with <indicators/evidence/assessments> in our classes. Be specific.*

SECTION 2 - DETERMINING OUR COURSE OF ACTION

OUR IDEAS: From our experiences, what are OUR ideas about the professional learning that we need?

RESEARCH-BASED IDEAS: What does the research say in terms of strategies that can impact student/educator learning in this area? (Possible sources might include sites such as www.bestevidence.org and https://educationendowmentfoundation.org.uk/evidence-summaries/teaching-learning-toolkit

PRACTICE-BASED IDEAS: What are other examples in different schools or contexts where this approach is demonstrating impact that we can learn from?

©FIRST EDUCATIONAL RESOURCES 2019

SECTION 3 - INCLUDING THE ELEMENTS OF EFFECTIVE PROFESSIONAL LEARNING

Effective Professional Learning Elements: *"In order for this to be successful, we know that PD needs to have the following elements. Check all that apply."*

- ○ Has a focus on the competency through our content
- ○ Is experiential in nature/allows us to learn by doing
- ○ Supports collaboration, specifically in job-embedded contexts
- ○ Requires us to create artifacts/products of our learning

- ○ Offers opportunities for feedback and requires reflection
- ○ Is longitudinal/takes place over time
- ○ Is developmental—it meets our educators where they are at
- ○ Has impact that can be observed

Comments:

SECTION 4- CREATING OUR ACTION STATEMENT — *"If we do…then we will observe…"*

Action Statement: If we do <initiative method/approach/pedagogy from Section 2> then we will observe <specific and visible changes to our practice we want to see>. Be specific.

SECTION 5 - DETERMINING OUR READINESS FOR THIS LEARNING

Readiness: *"How does this address our specific context?"* Mark each slider with an *"X"* to assess each readiness factor.

Our Context/Factors to be considered in this area:

A. Connection: We WANT to do this - it solves an instructional problem for us and our students in our classrooms

Low |- - - - - - - - - - - -| High

Comments:

B. Accountability: We NEED to do this - we will hold each other to working on this and will make our learning visible.

Low |- - - - - - - - - - - -| High

Comments:

C. Accessibility: We CAN do this - we have the resources and the capability to do sustained work in this area.

Low |- - - - - - - - - - - -| High

Comments:

SECTION 6 - OUR PLAN—FIRST STEP/NEXT STEPS/WHO CAN HELP

PLC 2.0 Toolkit

©FIRST EDUCATIONAL RESOURCES 2019

Professional Learning For Observable Impact Tool

This tool helps departments and grade level groupings develop a research-based and "do-able" professional learning plan that can be assessed for it's impact on classroom practice.

Prep time: 2 minutes to photocopy Planning for Observable Impact - Professional Learning Protocol

Time for Activity: 60 mins

Use this protocol to have your collaborative team:
- determine an instructional struggle point that they would like to learn more about.
- create a hypothesis of a descriptive and visible set of characteristics/features that would be demonstrated by students, educators and activities as a result of professional learning ("If we … then we will observe …").
- assess the research-base for the professional learning plan.
- determine readiness and first steps for the professional learning plan.

Things You Will Need:
- Professional Learning for Observable Impact Tool
- Post-It notes (two different colors like green and yellow), pens
- access to the internet for searching (laptops/Chromebooks/iPads/phones)

Part 1

Determining The Elements of Effective Professional Learning (15 minutes)

1. The team leader begins with a primer activity and asks the group, "Think of the worst professional learning that you ever had. What did that look like for you? Write down 5-7 characteristics of really poor professional learning, each on their own green Post-It note." (3 minutes)
2. The team leader then asks the group, "Think of the MOST HIGHLY IMPACTFUL professional learning that you ever had. What did that look like for you? Write down

5-7 characteristics of that exceptional professional learning experience, each on their own yellow Post-It note. (3 minutes)

3. The team then takes their green (bad professional learning) Post-it notes to a wall or flat surface and begins to place them up on the wall one by one in an Affinity Cluster (see Vision of a Learner Protocol (Part 1)).

   a. Lining up single file, participants place their Post-It notes up on a wall or flat surface. If the sticky is the same or similar (IE. 'no team norms' and 'team members speaking out of turn') to others that are up on the wall, the next participant places theirs close to the similar ones--different Post-Its (ie. 'no team norms' and 'lack of agenda') are placed farther apart. (2 minutes)

4. On a different space on the wall, the team places their yellow Post-It notes in the same fashion. (2 minutes)

5. The team looks at the Affinity Clusters and discusses what they notice. (5 minutes)

   a. The team leader refers them to Section 3 and says, "How does our list compare to the research-based characteristics in Section 3?"

Part 2

Naming the Instructional Challenge (7-10 minutes)

1. The team leader brings group to focus by saying, "Now that we have determined what effective and research-based professional learning looks like, it's time for us to look one of our instructional challenges and begin to plan for our professional learning in <attribute area decided by collaborative team>."

   a. The attribute should be taken from the school or department's Vision of a Learner.

2. The team leader reminds the group that while there are many factors that impact student learning, teaching has the largest impact, and that's where we will focus their attention.

   a. The team leader should encourage the group to acknowledge that when students are struggling in a certain area, the group should look for different ways to teach them.

   b. The team leader asks the group to name the instructional challenge with the framing "In <attribute in our area>, we struggle with teaching our students to…"

   c. Team leader gives an example: "In creative thinking in humanities, we struggle with teaching our students to think creatively when they are presented with a task that requires them to come up with a unique solution."

PLC 2.0 Toolkit

d. The group works on creating a sentence that names their instructional challenge.

3. Once the group has named the instructional challenge, the group determines their evidence this is a challenge with their students.
   a. The team leader reminds the group of the need to be specific with their evidence, as this evidence also begins to frame the success criteria.
   b. The group might vocalize things such as:
      i. "In our Urbanization unit, when we ask our students to design a city that highlights the positives and negatives of living in an urban center, most of our students produce something that looks very similar to the example they are given and/or to their friends. We also see this in other tasks that provide voice and choice."
   c. The team leader encourages the group to think of multiple tasks and assessments where they have observed students struggling with creative thinking.
      i. The team leader jots the ideas of the group down in the Building our Measures of Success box on the tool.

Part 3

Determining Our Course of Action (20 minutes)

1. The team leader asks the group to begin to brainstorm professional learning approaches the group can take to address the instructional challenge for the team. (5 minutes)
   a. The team leader jots down these ideas and asks for clarification and details as needed.
2. Once the ideas have been generated, the team leader asks the group to consider the research behind some of the suggested approaches. (10 minutes) The team leader can prompt the group using questions and tools such as:
   a. "We have so little professional learning time, we need to make sure that any time and effort we put in is time and effort well spent."
   b. "We want to make sure to avoid group-think mode where we just average opinions. It is vital that we use the research to support our thinking."
   c. The team leader can suggest visiting professional development sites such as www.bestevidence.org and https://educationendowmentfoundation.org.uk/evidence-summaries/teaching-learning-toolkit for more ideas.
3. The collaborative team then considers other departments in the school, schools, or districts they may be able to consult to get a peer/practice-based review. (5 minutes)

PLC 2.0 Toolkit

Part 4

Creating our Action Statement (15 minutes)

1. The team leader asks the group to consider the elements of effective professional learning from Section 3 in order to create an "If we … then we will observe …" Action Statement

    a. This statement is framed in the actions that the collaborative team will take (including structures, frequency of professional learning, supports, etc) and the results that they hope to see (one that positively changes teacher practice and improves student results).

    b. An example would be:

    "If we…

    - *participate in two full-day inservices spread over the year that…*
        - *has our collaborative team participate in activities that explicitly model and assess immersive creative thinking experiences,*
        - *has our collaborative team create tangible products from each of the inservices that allow us to make the products of our learning observable,*
        - *provides our collaborative team with specific tools and protocols that help them implement these critical thinking strategies and assess them in their classrooms,*
    - *use one collaborative period per month to…*
        - *use our collaborative team as year-long learning partners for ongoing observation, reflection and support around creative thinking strategies,*
        - *have our collaborative team present artifacts of our work over the course of the semester and reflect on the strengths and challenges of each of the creative thinking strategies,*

    Then we will observe…

    - *the products of our learning during each professional development session to guide our customized and developmental support for our team to effectively utilize creative thinking activities.*
    - *successes and challenges of each strategy to determine which strategies move us closer to our Vision of a Learner in creative thinking.*
    - *our students using these creative thinking strategies at a higher frequency in our classrooms."*

PLC 2.0 Toolkit

Part 5

Determining Our Readiness (5 minutes)
1. The team leader asks the group to look at the readiness factors to determine how:
   a. connected this learning will be to their context.
   b. whether they are willing to hold each accountable to this.
   c. whether they have the time and resources to do this.
2. The group reflects on the feasibility and reasonableness of the professional development plan.

Part 6

The Plan - First Steps/Next Steps/Who Can Help (5 minutes)
1. The team leader and the group outline:
   a. what needs to be done in the next 24 hours.
   b. what needs to be done in the next week.
   c. who is responsible for each action item.
   d. people and organizations that can be contacted for support.
   e. the date for the next meeting.
2. The Professional Learning for Observable Impact Tool is added to the Evidence Wall for the collaborative team.

Support Structures (Part 1) - Preparing For Impact

SUPPORT STRUCTURE (Circle one)   Staff Meeting   Department Meeting   Collaborative Meeting   PD Day   Other _____

SECTION A - LOW IMPACT

List the characteristics of this support if it was highly INEFFECTIVE and had LOW IMPACT. What might we observe participants DOING and DEMONSTRATING?

SECTION B - HIGH IMPACT

What is the OPPOSITE of each of these characteristics from COLUMN A? Write these highly EFFECTIVE characteristics below.

SECTION C - PRIORITIZE

Prioritize these characteristics in terms of creating a learning environment of observable impact for our participants in this structure.

SECTION D- SUPPORTS What are the specific supports that would enable our priorities for this structure?

SECTION E - OBSERVABLE IMPACT - If all of the elements from Section C and Section D were present, what what would we be capable of doing in this structure. What would we be able to DO and DEMONSTRATE? How would we know? What would be the products of our collaborative work together?

SECTION F - OUR ACTION STATEMENT - "With this support structure, if we…<from SECTION C> and enable these priorities by < from SECTION D>..then we will see participants <from SECTION E>.

SECTION G - SCHEDULING FOR REFLECTION - What are the DATES that we will revisit this document to determine whether we are having the observable impact we hoped?

©FIRST EDUCATIONAL RESOURCES 2019

PLC 2.0 Toolkit

58

Support Structures (Part 1) - Preparing For Impact

This tool builds a creative thinking routine to co-design a vision of a high-impact learning support structures (staff meetings, collaborative meetings, PD days, etc.).

Prep time: 2 minutes to photocopy Support Structures (Part 1) - Preparing for Impact Tool

Time for Activity: 40-50 mins

Use this protocol to have your collaborative team:
- use a creative thinking routine (creative inversion) that they can use in their classrooms.
- create a descriptive and observable set of characteristics/features of a high-impact meeting or support structure.
- design a testable hypothesis to determine the level of impact of the structure that they create.

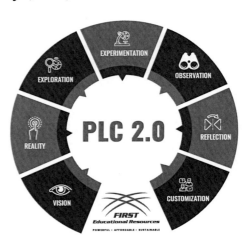

Things You Will Need:
- Copies of Support Structures (Part 1) - Preparing for Impact Tool
- Post-It notes, pens

Part 1

Creating the Vision - Structures for Impact (20 minutes)
1. Team leader begins by setting the stage for the group
   a. "Today we are going to be examining our <support structure (i.e. staff meetings)>. We are going to be creating a vision of what a high-impact structure looks like, the supports that will enable this structure to have the desired impact, and a testable action statement to see if it does what we hope this structure does for us."
2. The team leader distributes copies of the tool and gets the group into teams of three.
3. Team leader asks the groups "Think of the worst <staff meeting> that can picture. What does that look like for you? As a triad, write down 8-10 characteristics of a dreadful <staff meeting>, specifically what we would see participants DOING and

DEMONSTRATING.
   a. Write this in Section A for your small group. (3 minutes)
   b. The team leader encourages team to have fun with it, and to "go wild" with their thinking. (4 minutes)
4. The team leader asks small groups to share out and pick a few "gentler" characteristics and says, "Have we done any of these?" and asks the group to reflect on some of the current practices with this structure.
5. The team leader then says to the group, "Now, given what you have written, directly beside each characteristic of <a low impact and ineffective meeting>, write the opposite of that dreadful characteristic—this should reflect highly EFFECTIVE characteristics. (3 minutes)
6. The team leader asks small groups to share out and picks out a few positive characteristics and says' "Do we do any of these?" and asks the group to reflect on some of the current positive practices with this structure.
7. Prioritizing—The team leader asks the group to prioritize their lists, pick their top five characteristics, and write them on Post-It notes. (5 minutes)
   a. A member of each group then takes their top 5 to a large, flat surface in the room and places their Post-It Notes vertically, with their highest priority at the top and their lowest at the bottom.

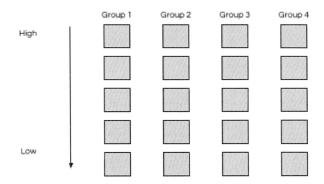

   b. Team leader and the group look at priorities and come to consensus on the ones that make the most sense for the context of the group.

Part 2

Envisioning the Possibilities (10 minutes)
1. The team leader brings group to focus saying, "Now that we have determined what this structure could look like, what are the supports that we would need to do this effectively? Be specific."
   a. The group brainstorms these supports and ensures that these supports are both attainable and sustainable.

PLC 2.0 Toolkit 60

       i.   Team leader encourages the group to consider not only the group who receives the supports, but also those who provide the support to make sure that it is do-able for all involved.

2. The team leader then asks the question, "If these supports were in place and our Priorities from Section C were present, what are the things that we would envision us DOING and DEMONSTRATING? What would we create that would make this structure one that has impact (changes our practice and improves student learning)? What might the products of our learning look like?"

    a. The small groups are given time to discuss/generate lists. (5 minutes)

3. OPTIONAL TWIST: The team leader pauses the group and says, "Now let's add the phrase "that you would observe us doing in the classroom" to each piece on our list. Do the products still fit?"

    a. Example, if the group were considering collaborative time, and one of the products was something like "rich discussion," the group would push the idea forward by saying, "How would we observe the products of our rich discussion in the classroom?"

Part 3

Creating our Action Statement - Planning For Impact (10 minutes)

1. Once the list of products from Step 3 above are generated, the team leader says, "By creating the products of this structure, we have actually generated a set of success criteria! It is our hope that if we enable our priorities, that we will be able to meet these criteria. But this is only a hypothesis -- also known as our ACTION STATEMENT.

2. The team leader asks each group to look at their Support Structures (Part 1) - Preparing For Impact Tool and create their own action statement using the stem provided in Section F:

    a. OUR ACTION STATEMENT - "With this support structure, if we ... <from SECTION C> and enable these priorities by < from SECTION D> ... then we will see participants <from SECTION E>."

3. Once each group has created an Action Statement, the statements are compared, and a final action statement is made.

    a. "This is the statement that we will look back on this structure later on in the <semester, year, etc> to determine whether it is having the impact that we have laid out in our success criteria. Can we agree on a date to revisit this statement?"

4. The group comes up with a date, and the team leader places this in Section G "Scheduling for Reflection" at the bottom of the form.

5. The completed Support Structures (Part 1) - Preparing For Impact form is added to the Evidence Wall for the group.

Support Structures (Part 2) - Reflecting On Impact

| SUPPORT STRUCTURE (Circle one) | Staff Meeting | Department Meeting | Collaborative Meeting | PD Day | Other _____ |

OUR ORIGINAL ACTION STATEMENT ABOUT THIS STRUCTURE: (FROM SUPPORT STRUCTURES, PART 1, SECTION F)

What are we noticing about this structure so far? What are we actually observing? WHEN an action (task, instruction, question) happened, THEN what happened? Are there any patterns we can learn from?

Reflect: Considering your Action Statement, what were the tasks, instructions, moves that led to the specific outputs that we hoped to see in our Action Statement? After each action, write (H) - high impact, (M) - medium impact, (L) - low impact, (N) - no impact/not sure

Learn: What should we continue to DO? What should we DO DIFFERENTLY?
CONTINUE TO DO: DO DIFFERENTLY:

SCHEDULING FOR REFLECTION - What are the DATES that we will revisit this document to monitor our observable impact with this structure?

PLC 2.0 Toolkit

©FIRST EDUCATIONAL RESOURCES 2019

Support Structures (Part 2) - Reflecting On Impact

This tool helps staff reflect on the impact of learning support structures (staff meetings, collaborative meetings, PD days, etc.).

Prep time: 7 minutes to
- photocopy Support Structures (Part 2) - Reflecting on Impact Tool
- obtain photocopies of the original Support Structures (Part 1) - Preparing For Impact Tool from the team evidence wall
- make three Post-It notes with the phrases "High Impact," "Medium Impact" and "Low Impact"

Time for Activity: 40-50 mins

Use this protocol to have your collaborative team:
- to analyze the level of impact of the structure that they created against their hypothesis for impact.
- to determine the tasks, instructions and specific strategies used with this structure that led to low, medium, and high levels of impact.
- to determine the next steps in terms of what needs to continue with this structure and what might need to be altered or discontinued.

Things You Will Need:
- copies of Support Structures (Part 2)- Reflecting on Impact Tool
- copies of the completed Support Structures (Part 1) - Preparing For Impact Tool filled out at a previous team meeting.
- Post-It notes, pens

Part 1

Re-Visiting our Action Statement (5-7 minutes)
1. Team leader begins by setting the stage for the group
   a. "Today we are going to be reflecting on the impact of our <support structure (i.e. staff meetings)> that we have observed since we last met about this

structure. If you recall, we co-created a vision of what a high impact version of this structure would look like using "creative inversion" as well as the supports that would enable this structure to have the impact that we hoped."

      i.   The team leader reminds the team that creative inversion is the protocol, where we designed the worst structure possible and then flipped it to become the best structure possible

          1.   The team leader asks if anyone used the strategy with their students and how it went.

   b.   "We also created our Action Statement as a hypothesis to test and see if this structure <i.e. staff meeting, collaborative meeting, etc> would have the impact that we hoped for. Today is the day that we had selected to reflect upon this structure as a group and see how it went according to our Action Statement."

   c.   Team leader distributes copies of the original Support Structures (Part 1) - Preparing For Impact Tool from the team evidence wall for each team member.

2.   The team looks at the Action Statement from Section F, which would look like

   a.   OUR ACTION STATEMENT - "With this support structure, if we...<from SECTION C> and enable these priorities by < from SECTION D>..then we will see participants <from SECTION E>."

   b.   The team then looks at Section E to ensure that everyone is familiar with what the original hypothesis about this structure was and what the group hoped this structure would help them do and demonstrate.

   c.   The team leader then gives the team two minutes to reflect on the support structure and how it met the criteria laid out in the Action Statement.

      i.   The team is encouraged to do this silently - there will be plenty of time to converse later in the protocol.

Part 2

Naming the Observations (5-7 minutes)

1.   The team leader then asks individuals to make their thinking visible by writing a minimum of five 'When ... then ..." statements to specifically describe what they have observed about the structure since the last time the team met about it.

   a.   EXAMPLE: "When we co-created team norms and reviewed them at every collaborative meeting, then I noticed that each of the team members followed the norms and contributed to the collaborative discussion."

   b.   Each observation is written on a separate Post-It note.

   c.   This exercise is done silently.

PLC 2.0 Toolkit

Part 3

Reflecting on Impact (15 minutes)

1. Once the team has created their "When ... Then ..." statements, the team leader places the three Post-It notes labeled "High Impact," "Medium Impact" and "Low Impact" in continuum fashion along a flat surface in the collaborative area, and asks the team to place each of their "When ... then ..." statements along that continuum.
   a. A high impact observation is defined as one that moved us closer to our ideal vision for this structure.
      i. If something has a large negative impact, it is placed on the Low Impact end of the continuum—it didn't move us closer to our vision.
   b. The team members ask for clarification on any of the sticky notes they might have questions about or that might need more specificity.
2. The team leader then asks the team to come to consensus on the placement of the "When ... then ..." statements saying, "Let's put these in order from what we think are the most impactful things that occured to the least impactful things that occurred according to our Action Statement, so we can begin to connect our actions to the impact we saw. No two statements can be equal; they each need their own spot on the continuum."
   a. The team moves any statements as needed until consensus is reached by the group.
   b. The team leader records the high, medium, and low impact statements on the master sheet for the collaborative team.
3. Once this clarification process has been completed, the team stands back and examines the continuum, and the team leader asks "What are we noticing?"
   a. The group begins to unpack any trends they see.

Part 4

Team Learning (15 minutes)

1. The team leader asks the team to look at the statements and asks, "Given our Action Statement and the impact that we had hoped we would have achieved with this structure, what should we...
   a. continue to do? Why? (5 minutes)
   b. do differently? Why? (5 minutes)
   c. What might we advise another team or school to do to enable the success of a structure like this?
   d. What are our next steps? When will we revisit this structure to see if we have been able to implement some of our 'do's' and 'do differently's'"?

2. The group comes up with a date, and the team leader places this in Scheduling for Reflection box at the bottom of the form, which is then added to the team Evidence Wall.

Rapid Research Jigsaw Tool

Department/Collaborative Team: _____   **Grade Level/Grouping/Subject (IE. Grade 6 math):** _____

INSTRUCTIONAL CHALLENGE: We struggle with our students being able to demonstrate:

POTENTIAL STRATEGY:

OUR PRIOR KNOWLEDGE: What do WE already know about this?

BEST AVAILABLE RESEARCH: What can we learn from the research that is available?

OTHER DEPARTMENT/SCHOOL/PEER REVIEWS: What can we learn from our colleagues in other contexts?

IMPACT RATING: LOW / MODERATE / HIGH

RAPID RESEARCH OVERALL RATING: This strategy has the potential for _____ impact in addressing our instructional challenge

POTENTIAL STRENGTHS OF THIS STRATEGY:

POTENTIAL CHALLENGES WITH THIS STRATEGY:

NEXT STEPS: As a result of our rapid research, our team recommendation is...

©FIRST EDUCATIONAL RESOURCES 2019

Rapid Research Jigsaw Tool

This tool helps collaborative teams do a rapid research scan of a new strategy to determine if it has potential for positive impact on a learning challenge.

Prep time: 5-10 minutes to photocopy this tool, and to gather any relevant information, handouts or websites that can inform the team about the strategy or approach in question

Time for Activity: 60 minutes

Use this protocol to have your collaborative team:
- examine a strategy or approach to collaboratively determine its potential to address an instructional challenge.
- utilize a "jigsaw" thinking routine to utilize the collective research powers of the group become rapid experts on the strategy or approach in question.

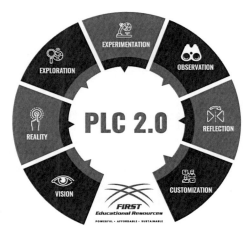

Things You Will Need:
- a copy of the Rapid Research Jigsaw Tool for each participant
- a description (electronic or paper, dependent on the needs of the team) that informs participants about the strategy in question
- access to the internet for each team member, preferably with a laptop

Part 1

Setting The Stage (3-5 minutes)
1. The team leader starts by saying "In the past couple of weeks, our team came to consensus about an instructional challenge that we are having. We find we are having an instructional challenge with <outcome, attribute>..."
    a. *Example: "We find that we are having an instructional challenge with our students able to consistently solve multi-step word problems in intermediate math independently of adult assistance."*
2. "This afternoon during our meeting, we are going to be examining <name of strategy or approach>, a strategy that appears to have some promise in allowing us to address

PLC 2.0 Toolkit   68

this challenge that we are having."
   a. *Example: 'collaborative problem solving'*
   b. The team leaders pauses, and allows the team to bring any questions forward to get clarity about the strategy.
3. The team leader or team member who brought the potential solution forward can highlight where they heard about the strategy and why it seems to have some promise in addressing the instructional challenge.
   a. *Example: "At the recent math conference, I spoke to Jane (a teacher from the neighboring district). She was having a similar challenge and said this had made a positive difference in their students' ability to solve problems on their own or in small groups."*
4. The instructional challenge and the strategy are written on the "master" Rapid Research Jigsaw Tool.

Part 2

Accessing Team Knowledge (7-10 minutes)

1. The team leader asks the group to consider the strategy in question (*ie. collaborative problem solving*) and says, "What do we know about this strategy? Where have we tried it in our own classrooms? Where have we seen it be successful? And given what you know, what might be your initial rating of this strategy in terms of its potential for impact--low, medium or high?
   a. The team jots their thoughts down silently in the Our Prior Knowledge box on the Rapid Research Jigsaw Tool.
      i. Each team member also circles their initial impact rating.
      ii. After two minutes, the team leader brings people's thoughts together through using a "last word" thinking routine.
         1. First team member reads their section on prior knowledge, then each team member gets 30-60 seconds to respond (depending on the size of the group), until all team members have made a comment.
         2. The first team member gets to speak last to summarize the thinking.
   b. This is repeated for each team member, and the team leader synthesizes the group dialogue on the master Rapid Research Jigsaw Tool for the team.
2. The team leader reads the synthesis and asks the team if that reflects the initial sentiments of the group.
3. Finally, the team leader asks each team member how they ranked the potential of this strategy, and the group comes to consensus on an initial impact rating in the Our Prior

Knowledge section.

    a. "This does not need to be contentious—this is just our initial feeling, which may change after we consider other sources of information about this strategy."

Part 3

Considering Other Practical Sources (3-5 minutes)

1. The team leader asks the collaborative group to switch gears and consider where they might have seen this strategy or a similar strategy utilized in different departments, contexts, or schools.

    a. "Where have we seen this used? Are there other departments or grade level groupings here in the school or in another school that are experiencing a similar instructional challenge that might be able to provide us some practical insights? Or in neighboring schools that we might be able to reach out to?"

2. The team has an open discussion about other educators or contexts that could provide useful information or authentic reviews on the strategy.

    a. The team leader reminds the group that this is not about whether someone liked or disliked the strategy; the group should constantly be considering the strategy's potential for impact on the instructional challenge.

3. The team leader jots down some ideas from the group.

4. The group will fill in the impact rating for Other Department/School/Peer Reviews section.

Part 4

Going Beyond our Collaborative Team - Peer and Research Reviews (15 minutes)

1. The team leader says, "It's also helpful for us to access any information that we might be able to gather outside of our collaborative team. If we are going to spend time on this strategy, we need to make sure that the research says that it actually has a chance to make a difference to our instructional challenge and has a high return on our efforts."

2. The team informs the group that they are going to become a research team, and for the next 20 minutes, the team is going to open up <laptops, tablets> and begin to look at sources of research and/or peer reviews that might be able to help.

    a. The goal is for each team member to find different sources of information, and to create a "headline" of 20 words or less that summarizes an article or study.

        i. Each team member should try to get three headlines from their research.

    b. Sample research sites include:

PLC 2.0 Toolkit   70

i. Educational Endowment Foundation https://educationendowmentfoundation.org.uk (has strategies, costs, and strength of evidences ratings)

ii. Visible Learning https://visible-learning.org/hattie-ranking-influences-effect-sizes-learning-achievement/ A summary of the work of John Hattie and Visible Learning

iii. ERIC https://eric.ed.gov/? Searchable education journal/article database

Part 5

Research Headlines (10 minutes)

1. Team leader asks for the group to prioritize their headlines in terms of the headline's importance in informing the group about the strategy.
   a. Blockbuster—headlines that might surprise, shock and amaze the group.
   b. Newsworthy—headlines that are important to hear.
   c. Much Ado About Nothing—headlines that don't add new information to the team discussion.
2. Each team member shares their research or peer review headlines using Comment, Question, Ditto, Pass thinking routine
   a. Each team member shares one headline, and the team leader gives each group member 30 seconds to either comment, question, ditto (it's already been said) or pass.
3. This process is repeated until all Blockbuster and Newsworthy headlines are covered.
4. Team leader says, "As a result of our research, what impact rating would we give this strategy if we were to consider what we have discovered from:
   a. other departments/school/peer reviews.
   b. best available research?"
5. Each team member fills out their potential impact rating (low, moderate or high) for those two sections, and the group comes to consensus in those two categories.
   a. These are recorded on the master sheet by the team leader.

Part 6

Strengths/Challenges/Final Review/Next Steps (5-7 minutes)

1. The team leader asks each group member to silently consider one potential strength and one potential challenge that they found as a result of their research and the resultant discussions.
   a. The potential strengths are shared one at a time, followed by potential

PLC 2.0 Toolkit

challenges one at a time, and recorded by the team leader.

2. The team leader then asks, "Given our knowledge, the knowledge of our peers, the best available research, and the potential strengths or challenges, what would be our Rapid Research Overall Rating?
    a. The team is asked to silently write their overall rating on their sheet.
    b. The team leader asks each team member to share, one at a time in rapid fire fashion, and then asks, "What did we hear?"
        i. The team comes to consensus on whether this strategy has a low, moderate, or high level of potential to address the instructional challenge that was named by the team.
            1. This can be done by discussion or by giving an average numerical values based on everyone's rating. Use the following numeric values:
                a. "Low" = 1
                b. "Moderate" = 2
                c. "High" = 3

3. The final review is recorded on the master, and the team decides on the next course of action.
    a. This could range from…
        i. Moving forward with the strategy and adding details to move ahead.
        ii. Gathering more information with thoughts on who to contact and where to look to get a more fulsome picture of the strategy.
        iii. Looking for a different approach and picking a date to visit a new possible approach.

4. The decision is recorded on the master Rapid Research Jigsaw Tool and placed on the collaborative team Evidence Wall.

PLC 2.0 Toolkit

Attribute Analysis Tool - At/Need To Go

Use this tool to determine your current attribute profile and future work that will allow your team to have a complete picture of one of your areas of focus in your Vision of a Learner and to prioritize your actions going forward.

Department/Collaborative Team: _____ **Grade Level/Grouping/Subject (IE. Grade 6 math):** _____

Our Attribute/Focus: _____

ANALYZING OUR CURRENT PROFILE FOR THIS ATTRIBUTE/AREA OF FOCUS

	STUDENTS WOULD BE:	EDUCATORS WOULD BE:	ACTIVITIES/ASSESSMENTS WOULD BE:	SUPPORTS WOULD BE:
STEP 1: What would we observe each of the following groups DOING and DEMONSTRATING, or the enabling structures/supports DOING to lead to a high level of proficiency in this attribute focus area.				
STEP 2: What are our STRENGTHS in this area and or what are we doing in this area that allows us to effectively observe students demonstrating this characteristic?				
STEP 3: Where do we need to go in this area to help us observe students demonstrate this attribute at a high level of proficiency?				
Step 4: Our Next Steps				

STEP 5: Prioritizing Our Next Steps ➔

©FIRST EDUCATIONAL RESOURCES 2019

PLC 2.0 Toolkit

STEP 5: Prioritizing Our Next Steps - From Step 4, place your next steps into one of the four quadrants below to help the team prioritize your next action steps.

Easier

	Zone 3: Easier to implement and lower impact	Zone 4: Easier to implement and higher impact
Ease of Implementation		
	Zone 1: More difficult to implement and lower impact	Zone 2: More difficult to implement and higher impact

More difficult

Lower   **Potential Level of Impact**   Higher

STEP 6: Prioritized next steps to best enable the demonstration of this attribute in our area -

©FIRST EDUCATIONAL RESOURCES 2019

PLC 2.0 Toolkit

74

Attribute Analysis Tool At/Need To Go

This tool helps collaborative teams to look at their current level of progress in an attribute area and prioritize their next steps.

Prep time: 7 mins - 5 mins to photocopy protocol and find chart paper, markers and Post-It notes, and two minutes to create the priority diagram on the chart paper

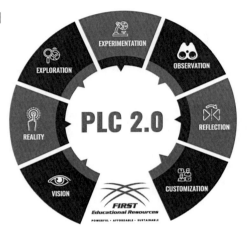

Time for Activity: 55-60 minutes

Use this protocol to have your collaborative team or group:
- assess where their current strengths and areas of need in terms of...
    - what their students are currently DOING and DEMONSTRATING in this area of focus.
    - what the collaborative team is currently DOING and DEMONSTRATING in terms of their teaching in this area of focus.
    - what their activities and assessments are currently having their students DO and DEMONSTRATE.
    - what their support structures are currently enabling the team and their students to DO and DEMONSTRATE.
- to prioritize next steps in terms of level of potential impact of the action and its ease of impact for the collaborative team.

Things You Will Need:
- copies of the Attribute Analysis Tool - At/Need To Go Tool for each participant
- the current departmental and/or school VIsion of a Learner
    - (NOTE: If there is no current vision, no problem! It just means you will have to adjust the timelines for this activity, and you may have to do it over multiple meetings)
- Post-It notes, markers, large piece of chart paper
    - chart paper set up into four labeled quadrants like Page 2, Step 5 of the Attribute Analysis Tool - At/Need To Go (see diagram on next page)

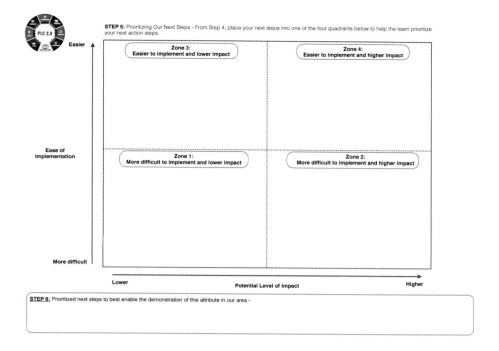

- OPTIONAL: copy of the departmental and/or school Vision of a Learner

Part 1

Clarifying the Vision (15 minutes)
1. Team leader starts by saying, "This afternoon during our meeting, we are going to be determining our current level of progress on one of the attributes from our department/school Vision of a Learner. The goal of today's meeting is for our collaborative team to get a sense of where we are at and to prioritize where we need to go next through two lenses: the level of impact of the action and its ease of implementation."
    a. "We all know how busy we are, so we want to see what some of the 'low hanging fruit' might be in this attribute area as well as where we want to focus our team efforts going forward."
2. The team leader asks the group to write the attribute in question into the tool (i.e. creative thinking in intermediate English) and says, "In our department/grade grouping, what would we observe students doing and demonstrating if they were at a high level of proficiency in this area?" (3 minutes)
    a. The group brainstorms (and refers to the departmental/school Vision of a Learner, if developed).
    b. The team leader jots down the ideas from the group, encouraging them to be specific and to avoid jargon ("What would someone who has never been to one of our classes see? How would they know?").

PLC 2.0 Toolkit

c. Each of the group members jots these features down in the column under Step 1 of the Attribute Analysis Tool - At/Need To Go Tool.
1. This process is repeated...
   a. For educators (3 minutes)—"What would someone observe us doing if we were teaching this in a way that allowed for a high level of proficiency for our students?"
      i. i.e. "What would we be doing and demonstrating if we were teaching and modeling creative thinking in intermediate English?"
   b. For classroom activities and assessments (3 minutes)—"What would the types of activities and assessments look like that allowed ALL of our students to demonstrate creative thinking in our classes?"
   c. For supports (3 minutes)—"What do we need to do this? What would empower us?"
      i. The team leader encourages the team to be very specific. For example, if the team said "time," the group's response should be "Time to do what? What would we be creating in this time? What would we observe as the products of our learning?"

Part 2

Examining Our Current Evidence of Strengths (10 minutes)

1. The team leader asks the collaborative group to then consider each of the areas from Step 1 (students, educators, activities/assessments and supports) and says, "As a collaborative team, we always want to start with our strengths, so in each of these areas, what are we currently doing that affords us the opportunity to observe students demonstrating these things at a high level of proficiency?"
   a. The team leader asks the group to be extremely specific, and the team pushes each other with statements such as "Let's be more specific," "We say that, but what are we observing that tells us that is actually occurring?" and "How do we know that?"
2. The team members share their thoughts and evidence, and they write these things in the column under Step 2.

Part 3

Determining our Gaps and Brainstorming Where We Need to Go (10 minutes)

3. The team leader asks the collaborative group to then consider each of the areas from Step 1 (students, educators, activities/assessments and supports), and says, "Given our strengths, where are the gaps? Where do we need to go in each of these areas?"

77   *PLC 2.0 Toolkit*

a. The team leader again asks the group to be extremely specific, but also to think beyond what the group currently does. The group is encouraged to get as many ideas down as they can.
  i. "There are no bad ideas at this point; let's just get them out there and see where it leads!"
  ii. The team is encouraged to feed ideas forward, using a "Yes! And we could …" approach to add to the ideas of the team rather than a "No, we couldn't do that …" approach that shuts down further creative thinking.
4. The team members share their thoughts and ideas, and they write these in the column under Step 3.

Part 4

Turning Ideas to Action (5 minutes)

1. The team leader distributes Post-It notes to each of the group members, and the group takes the ideas that are written beside each of students, educators, activities/assessments and supports and turns them into actions.
  a. "What would be the steps that we need to take these ideas and make them a reality?"
  b. Team members jot the individual actions on Post-It notes.

Part 5

Prioritizing our Next Steps (10 minutes)

1. The team leader says, "We have so many actions here, and so little time! We know how busy we are, and how much time we can actually commit to this. Given the time that we feel we need to spend on this attribute area in our context, we must prioritize the actions that we came up with in our brainstorm in terms of their…
  a. potential level of impact.
  b. ease of implementation.
2. The team leader then refers to the large chart paper set up on the wall from Step 5 and asks the team to begin to place their Post-It notes in the quadrant that they feel that action fits best.
  a. Once all of the Post-It notes are up on the wall, the team members are asked to take a marker and put a star on any sticky they feel might be better placed in a different quadrant.
3. The team discusses any starred Post-It note, and tries to come to consensus on where that strategy should finally sit.
4. With any strategy, the team asks questions such as, "I wonder what the research

PLC 2.0 Toolkit

would tell us about that strategy/action?" or "Who else is doing work in this area, and what might we learn from them?"

Part 6

Learning/Prioritized Next Steps (5 minutes)

1. Team leader asks for the group to reflect on the activity.
   a. "What have we learned about our next steps in this attribute area? What do we need to continue doing? What might we need to change? What are our next steps?"
2. The team leader asks the team to be specific in terms of next steps, who needs to be involved, and when they will reconnect to check on progress and reassess.
3. The completed tool is placed on the collaborative team Evidence Wall.

Engaging Task Generator

In PLC 2.0, is is vital that our students learn our collaboratively determined "High Priority Outcomes": our curricular outcomes that are vital to learn and allow us to observe our students doing and demonstrating the attributes that make up our vision of a learner. In order to ensure these outcomes are learned, we need to make the most engaging task sequences possible for our learners through determining how they learn best, their prior knowledge, and the elements of engaging lessons for today's learner. Use this tool with your collaborative team to brainstorm your high impact learning sequences.

Department/Collaborative Team: _____ **Date:** _____

Attribute from our Vision of a Learner:

High Priority Outcomes (Curricular outcomes that are vital to learn AND give us the opportunity to teach and assess this attribute:

OPTION: THE NEW STRATEGY WE ARE TRYING:

SECTION 1: OUR LEARNERS - What do we know about our learners?

Consider the learner in our context and when the learner is most engaged: "These learners learn best when they are _____ "

What is the PRIOR KNOWLEDGE and PRIOR ATTITUDES of our students about this topic? How do we know? What (other) actions do we need to take to find out?

SECTION 2: OUR VISION - What would we see if these outcomes were done well?

IN OUR STUDENTS: What would you observe students DOING and DEMONSTRATING in their classrooms. Be as specific as you can - what would you see and hear?

IN OUR TASK DESIGN: What are the types of tasks that would require students to DO and DEMONSTRATE this attribute? How would they be designed? What might the products look like? What would be the style and types of questions that might be used?

PLC 2.0 Toolkit

©FIRST EDUCATIONAL RESOURCES 2019

80

BRAINSTORM - Given what we know about our learner and the learning that we want to see, what are the possible tasks that would allow us to observe our students demonstrating this outcome.

ENGAGEMENT BOOSTER - How might we make this even more relevant to our learner?

NOTES/IDEAS

CONNECTIVITY FACTOR (I want to do this!)

Check Applicable   Doing   Do More

- Connects to their prior learning
- The learner it needs now, or in the near future
- Makes something easier/saves the learner time
- Relates to something the learner is already doing
- Impacts something that is important to the learner
- Provides feedback to the learner

ACCOUNTABILITY FACTOR ("I need to do this!")

Doing   Do More

- Requires thinking to be made visible
- Requires conversation
- Requires creation of a product
- Requires iteration of the product
- Requires presentation of the product
- Requires utilization of the product

ACCESSIBILITY FACTOR ("I can do this!")

Doing   Do More

- Learner-friendly language
- Concepts chunked into manageable bits
- Connects to the learner through analogy/symbols/patterns
- Utilizes familiar images/symbols/patterns
- Allows for self-pacing and mastery
- Allows for voice and choice

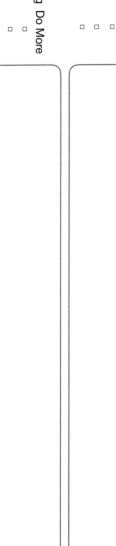

NEW LEARNING DESIGN/NEXT STEPS:

©FIRST EDUCATIONAL RESOURCES 2019

PLC 2.0 Toolkit

Engaging Task Generator

This tool helps collaborative teams create engaging, learner-centered tasks to help students learn our highest priority outcomes and demonstrate attributes of our Vision of a Learner.

Prep time: 5 mins to photocopy this protocol

Time for Activity: 60 minutes

Use this protocol to have your collaborative team:
- look an upcoming unit and develop engaging task sequences that are…
    - are connected to students' prior learning and contexts.
    - are highly accessible.
    - hold students accountable to their learning.
- to examine whether our current attribute assessment profile allows us to observe our students demonstrating this attribute at a high level of proficiency, or if there are adjustments that we can make to accurately observe our students' abilities in this attribute area.

Things You Will Need:
- copies of the Engaging Task Generator Tool for each participant
- high-priority outcomes from an upcoming unit for the collaborative group
- OPTIONAL: copy of the departmental and/or school Vision of a Learner

Part 1

Setting The Stage (5 minutes)
1. Team leader starts by saying, "This afternoon during our meeting, we are going to be generating ideas for creating engaging task sequences that best allow us to observe <enter attribute, i.e. critical thinking> and learn our high priority outcomes in our upcoming unit on <enter unit> here."
2. The team leader asks the group to list the high priority outcomes for the upcoming unit on the Engaging Task Generator Sheet.
3. OPTION: if the collaborative team is trying a new strategy (i.e. using opinion lines or using visual organizers to assist critical thinking), they would insert that in the Option box.

PLC 2.0 Toolkit

Part 2

Considering Our Learners (15 minutes)

1. The team leader encourages the group to begin their task sequence design by considering the learner.
    a. The group might discuss what "today's learner" looks like in their classroom.
    b. The team leader can ask questions like, "When DO we see our learners engaged? What can we learn from those times when they are engaged?"
        i. The team fills in the box with "These learners learn best when …" with specific, learner-centered details. (3-5 minutes)
2. The team leader reminds the collaborative group that one of the most important, research-supported structures for success is building on the prior knowledge of students, and the team leader then asks:
    a. "What do our students already know about this topic, or topics that are similar to this that we would have already taught?"
    b. "How might they be feeling about this topic?"
    c. "What actions might we need to take to determine their prior learning?"
        i. Team fills in Prior Knowledge and Attitudes box. (3-5 minutes)
3. The team leader then asks the group to consider the attribute in question and says, "In our department/grade grouping, what would we observe students doing and demonstrating if they were at a high level of proficiency in this area?" (3 minutes)
    a. The group brainstorms and refers to the Departmental Vision of a Learner (if developed).
    b. Team leader jots down the ideas from the group, encouraging them to be specific and to avoid jargon using questions like, "What would someone who has never been to one of our classes see? How would they know?"
    c. Each of the group members jots these features down in the In Our Learners box.
4. The team leader asks the collaborative group to switch gears and consider the attribute lens from a different perspective—the tasks/assessments perspective. (3-5 minutes)
    a. "If this is what we would want to see students doing and demonstrating in this attribute area, what are the types of activities and assessments that allow us to observe each of our learners demonstrating this attribute at a high level of proficiency?"
        i. These are written into the In Our Task Design box.

83   *PLC 2.0 Toolkit*

Part 3

Brainstorming (20 minutes)

1. The team leader "turns the group loose" and says, "Given what we know about our learners, how they learn best, their prior knowledge and the tasks that we want to create so we can observe their learning, what ideas can we come up with that allow our students to learn what WE would want to do if we were them?"
2. Team is split into small groups, and they brainstorm ideas for task sequences.
3. After 15 minutes, the group is brought back together to share ideas they have had about the task sequence.
   a. The team leader encourages the group to think of "warms and wonders" (positive feedback and challenging questions) based on their ideas.
4. The team tries to come up with 3-4 promising ideas for task sequences they would be willing to try with their students in these high priority outcome areas.

Part 4

Boosting Engagement of Our Tasks (10 minutes)

1. The team leader then asks the group to run their ideas through the "Engagement Booster" on the Engaging Task Tool to check three factors:
   a. CONNECTIVITY FACTOR (I want to do this!)
   b. ACCOUNTABILITY FACTOR ("I need to do this!")
   c. ACCESSIBILITY FACTOR ("I can do this!")
2. The team takes each of the ideas that were created in Part 3 and looks to see what the task is 'doing' in each of these areas, and what it might need to 'do more of' in these areas, while they jot down ideas about how the task sequence might be made to be even more engaging for their learner.

Part 5

New Learning Design (5-10 minutes)

1. The team leader then asks the collaborative group to consolidate their ideas into a new learning design, and the group reflects upon the process and assigns next steps to develop the engaging learning task for the high-priority outcomes for the upcoming unit.
2. Sample tasks are placed on the collaborative team Evidence Wall.

PLC 2.0 Toolkit

Classroom Observation Tool

Vision of a Learner Attribute/Element: _____   Strategy/Task: _____

CREATING OUR ACTION STATEMENT: "If we do…then we will observe…."

<u>Action Statement</u>: If we do <strategy/activity> then we will observe our students DOING and DEMONSTRATING <specific outputs we want to see>. Be specific in terms of what you might observe students saying, doing, creating.

NARROWING THE FOCUS: "LOOK FORS": Considering our action statement, what are we going to focus on?

<u>"NEED to Look For's"</u>   <u>"NICE to Look For's</u>:

DESCRIBING THE "ACTION"

<u>Action</u>: What did you observe in the classroom? What were the activities/teachings? What were learners doing and demonstrating? If you were able to ask them, what were the words kids were using? Use descriptive language to paint the instructional picture.

<u>Activities/Teaching/Talk</u>   <u>Doing/Demonstrating</u>

©FIRST EDUCATIONAL RESOURCES 2019

85

PLC 2.0 Toolkit

DESCRIBING THE "ACTION" - CONTINUED

Action: What did you observe in the classroom? What were the activities/teachings? What were learners doing and demonstrating? If you were able to ask them, what were the words kids were using? Use descriptive language to paint the instructional picture.

Activities/Teaching/Talk

Doing/Demonstrating

CONNECTING ACTIONS TO RESPONSES (Creating "When...then..." statements)

"WHEN ......"

"THEN ......"

Learn: Next time, what will I continue to DO? What will we DO DIFFERENTLY?

DO:

DO DIFFERENTLY:

PLC 2.0 Toolkit

©FIRST EDUCATIONAL RESOURCES 2019

Classroom Observation Tool

This tool helps members of collaborative teams to prepare for effective, descriptive self- or peer-observations of an activity sequence or lesson.

Prep time: 2 mins to photocopy the Classroom Observation Tool

Time for Activity: 30-35 minutes

Use this protocol to have your collaborative team:
- set a focus for observing the impact of their activity sequence.
- develop their descriptive observational skills.

Things You Will Need:
- copies of the Classroom Observation Tool for each participant
- a collaboratively developed strategy/activity sequence that will be tried in the next few days

Part 1

Setting the Stage (10 minutes)
1. The team leader welcomes the group and lets them know that today's meeting is aimed at answering the question: "How might we be able to descriptively observe a strategy we are planning to use in our classrooms to connect our actions to impact?"
2. The team leader asks the group, "When we consider <upcoming strategy/activity>, what do we hope to observe our students DOING and DEMONSTRATING?
    a. The group brainstorms a number of observations they might make using this strategy or activity sequence.
    b. The team leader encourages the team to be specific in terms of what they might hope to observe students saying, doing, and creating as a result of the strategy.
        i. "The more specific and descriptive we get, the easier it will be for us to know if we hit the mark with the strategy."
    c. EXAMPLE: Number talks to develop critical thinking for Grade 6 math
        i. "We would hear each of the students in the group discussing different aspects of the word problem."

ii. *"We would hear students justifying the methods they are using to try to solve the problem."*

iii. *"We would hear students saying things like 'I like that method because of...' and 'I hadn't thought of that strategy before.'*

iv. *"We would see groups of students writing multiple methods to solve the problem."*

v. *"We would see students making multiple attempts at the problem."*

d. The team then fills in the Action Statement.

Part 2

Narrowing the Focus (10 minutes)

1. The team leader tells the group that as much as we might want to see all of these things, we can only focus on so many things at once.

2. The team leader asks the group to prioritize their ideal observations into "need to look fors" and "nice to look fors."

   a. The team differentiates by asking, "What are the key things that we would observe that would tell us that this strategy is leading to the learning that we want?"

   b. The team determines two or three things that they will focus on during the observation.

3. The team leader asks the team to think about what they might see and how they might describe it and encourages them to be descriptive about what they see.

   a. "Rather than 'The kids seemed really engaged,' we need to ensure that we continuously ask ourselves, 'What am I seeing that makes me think that?'"

   b. "Rather than 'The kids seemed really engaged', how many students were participating in the activity? 7/20? 15/20?"

   c. "What were the students actually doing?"

   d. "When you listened to students, what were they saying? What were the types of questions that they were asking?"

   e. "When you asked students questions, how did they respond?"

Part 3

"When ... then ..." statements (10 minutes)

1. The team leader says, "The goal of our observations is to start to create 'When ... then ...' statements that come as a result of our actions in the classroom. When we are examining this new strategy, we want to see which teaching approaches lead to the learning that we want, and which teaching approaches do not, so that we can begin to

PLC 2.0 Toolkit

collect patterns across our classrooms."

    a. The team leader asks the team to review the new strategy or approach and asks them to create 4-5 predictive "When ... then ..." statements.

        i. The team leader says, "With a partner on the team, look over the learning design that we have created as a group. Try to come up with 4-5 "When ... then ..." statements that you think might occur at different points during the activity sequence."

        ii. After three minutes, the team puts forward their predictive "When ... then ..." statements and the group discusses why they might see some of those predictions and how the team might make those pieces better.

Part 4

Final Preparations for Observations (2 minutes)

1. The team leader reminds the team that doing observations (self or peer) is challenging, and the key is to jot down observations as often as possible, even if they are rough observations.

    a. "We can often get caught up with teaching, and that's what we should be doing! But we also want to be cognizant of what is happening as a result of our actions, so "over-observing" is a good thing. As a collaborative team, we will clean up the observations after we give the new strategy a try."

2. The floor is opened up for any final questions or thoughts prior to the lesson.

3. The team finishes by ensuring that their observation sheets are ready to go with their "need to look fors" and "nice to look fors" ready to guide their self or peer observations.

4. A copy of the Classroom Observation Tool with the Narrowing the Focus section completed is placed on the collaborative team Evidence Wall.

PLC 2.0 Toolkit

Observation-To-Impact Connection Protocol (TEAM)

Vision of a Learner Attribute/Element: _____ Strategy/Task: _____

Team Member: _____ Date: _____

REFLECTING ON OUR ACTIONS (Creating "When...then..." statements)

Part 1: What were your "When..Then..." statements from your observations of this strategy in your classroom? Write them below.

Part 2: Considering your "When…Then's", what were the actions, activities, instructions and/or teaching moves that led to one or more of the specific outputs that you hoped to see? After each action, write **(H)** - high impact, **(M)** - medium impact, **(L)** - low impact, **(N)** - no impact/not sure

Part 3: Write each of your "When…then's" and their impact level onto Post-It Notes

ESTABLISHING TRENDS - Affinity Clustering

Part 4: Have each team member line up, single file. Team Member #1 places their first "When…then…" statement on the wall. Team Member #2 follows: if their "When…then…" is similar, they place it next to the first statement. If it is different, they place it at a new region. All team members follow, one by one, placing their statements on the wall in similar fashion until 'affinity clusters' are created. What are the trends that our group notices? Write them below.

TEAM DISCUSSION

<u>Learn</u>: What are the actions that had the highest impact? How do we know? What have we learned about this strategy in terms of observable impact?
OPTION: Use "Get to The Root" of Impact - Root Cause Tool to go deeper into the "WHYs" of impact.

PLC 2.0 Toolkit

©FIRST EDUCATIONAL RESOURCES 2019

90

Observation to Impact Connection Tool (Team)
(Post-observation)

This tool helps members of collaborative teams unpack classroom observations and connect their actions to impact in the classroom.

Prep time: 5 mins to photocopy the Observation-to-Impact Connection Tool (TEAM), gather chart paper, markers and Post-It notes

Time for Activity: 45-55 minutes

Use this protocol to have your collaborative team:
- determine trends and patterns from classroom observation.
- connect their specific teaching moves and actions with a strategy or approach to responses from their students.

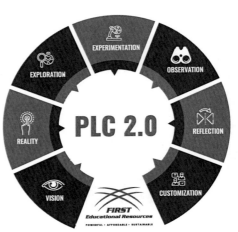

Things You Will Need:
- copies of completed Observation-to-Impact Connection Tool from each participant from a previously observed lesson
- Post-It notes, markers, large flat surface or poster paper

Part 1

Setting the Stage (10 minutes)
1. The team leader welcomes the group and lets them know that today's meeting is aimed at answering the question, "How can we use our observations to connect our actions to impact?"
2. The team leader asks the group to pull out their Classroom Observation Tool they filled out from their last lesson.
   a. The team leader says, "Everyone's thoughts are valuable, and you will likely recognize some of the patterns that you hear to be similar to those from your own classroom."
   b. Each team member looks at their observations and writes three "headline" of

20 words or less that summarizes their observations.

    c. Team leader asks for the group to prioritize their headlines in terms of the headline's importance in informing the group about the strategy

        i. Blockbuster—headlines that might surprise, shock and amaze the group.

        ii. Newsworthy—headlines that are important to hear.

        iii. Much Ado About Nothing—headlines that don't add new information to the team discussion.

Part 2

Considering your "When ... Then ..." Statements (15 minutes)

1. The team leader asks the group what were the actions, activities, instructions and/or teaching moves that led to one or more of the specific outputs that they hoped to see?

2. The team leader asks the group to write each of these "When ... then ... statements" on a Post-It note and indicate the level of impact they thought this action had by writing...

    a. (H) - high impact,

    b. (M) - medium impact,

    c. (L) - low impact, or

    d. (N) - no impact/not sure

3. Regardless of the level of impact, the team constantly asks themselves why they put it in the spot they did and are specific and descriptive in their responses.

Part 3

Looking for trends using Affinity Clustering (10 minutes)

1. Team leader has each team member line up, single file.

    a. Team Member #1 places their first "When ... then ..." statement on the wall.

    b. Team Member #2 follows. If their "When ... then ..." is similar, they place it next to the first statement. If it is different, they place it a new region.

    c. All team members follow, one by one, placing their statements on the wall in similar fashion until all Affinity Clusters are created.

2. Team leader asks, "What are the trends that our group notices?" The group discusses the trends and begins to consider the role of each of the following with the trends they have found.

    a. The student

    b. The teaching

    c. The activity or assessment itself

PLC 2.0 Toolkit

3. The team leader encourages the group to look through each of these lenses for each trend they are seeing, and the group constantly asks, "What other evidence can we recall that might help us determine impact?"

Part 4

Reflection/Learning from Trends (10-15 minutes)

1. Team leader says, "In looking at our patterns, what are the actions that had the highest impact? How do we know? What have we learned about this strategy in terms of observable impact?"
   a. OPTION: Use "Get To The Root" of Impact - Root Cause Tool to go deeper into the "WHYs" of impact.
2. The team creates a set of summary statements and determines one of three outcomes:
   a. "Our observations and patterns suggest this strategy/approach needs further investigation in order to determine its level of impact."
      i. This would be common after the first few attempts at this strategy or approach, or early on in the implementation cycle so that impact could be seen from a more longitudinal perspective.
   b. "Our observations and patterns suggest this strategy/approach does not need further investigation in order to determine its level of impact, and we should continue this practice because…."
      i. This would be followed with specific reviews that support continuing the practice.
   c. "Our observations and patterns suggest this strategy/approach does not need further investigation in order to determine its level of impact, and we should not continue this practice because…."
      i. This would be followed with specific reviews that support discontinuing the practice.
3. A copy of the Observation-To-Impact Connection Protocol (TEAM) is placed on the collaborative team Evidence Wall.

"Get To The Root" of Impact - Root Cause Tool

Part 1: BRAINSTORM - From your lesson, place a pattern that you observed (something students were DOING or DEMONSTRATING in the classroom that you are curious about) as a result of a teaching move or strategy in the centre and circle it. Then as a group, brainstorm reasons why that particular action might have had the level of impact that was observed. (5 minutes)

Part 2: GET TO THE ROOT: From your brainstorm above, pick two of your most promising potential reasons why the approach had the level of impact observed. Write each of those reasons at as a statement at the top of one of the columns below. Say the phrase, and then ask 'Why?'. Write the responses below each, and 'go deep' to get to the root of why you observed that level of impact. (2 minutes for each reason)

Reason: _____

- WHY?
- WHY?
- WHY?
- WHY?

Reason: _____

- WHY?
- WHY?
- WHY?
- WHY?

Part 3: REFLECT - What can we learn about having impact in this area? In other areas?

©FIRST EDUCATIONAL RESOURCES 2019

PLC 2.0 Toolkit

94

Get To The Root - Root Cause Analysis Tool

This post-observation tool helps teams move beyond "it worked" or "it didn't work" when collaboratively reflecting on a lesson, activity or approach.

Prep time: 2 mins to photocopy protocol

Time for Activity: 35-40 minutes

Use this protocol to have your collaborative team:
- develop a deeper understanding of their observations (self or group) of a lesson, activity sequence or approach.
- use the findings of a root cause analysis to guide future lesson design.

Things You Will Need:
- copies of the 'Get To The Root" of Impact - Root Cause Tool' for each participant
- each collaborative team member to bring copies of the completed master of the Observation To Impact Connection Protocol (Team)
- Post-it notes, markers

Part 1

Reconnecting with Our Classroom Observations (15 minutes)
1. The team leader begins by saying, "Today we are going to reflect upon observations that we have made around the <lesson, strategy, approach> that we tried so that we can begin to connect some of our actions to the impact that we observed in our classrooms when we did this activity."
    a. Team leader has the group pull out their Observation Sheets.
2. The team leader asks the group, "What did you notice when you tried this <lesson, strategy, approach> in your classroom. What were some of the things that you observed that impacted the trajectory of the lesson and the learning? Jot down your observations and remember to be specific and descriptive, as if you were a cameraman, not a journalist."
    a. The team jots down their observations. (5 minutes)

3. Quality Control—The team leader asks the team to get into partners to begin to look at their observations and to ensure that the observations are specific and descriptive. (5 minutes)
    a. If one of the observations needs more specificity, the partners should be asking questions like "What did you observe that made you think that?" (i.e. "The students were confused." vs. "When I gave the instruction, a large number of students were not able to start the task.")
4. The team leader asks the team to take their most promising observations to impact learning (either positive or negative impact) and place them on Post-It notes (4-5 observations per team member).
5. The team then takes their promising connections Post-it notes to a wall or flat surface and begins to place them up on the wall one by one in an Affinity cluster fashion (see Vision of a Learner Protocol (Part 1)).
    a. Lining up single file, one by one, participants place their Post-It notes up on a wall or flat surface.
        i. If there characteristic is similar, they place their characteristic close to the first one.
        ii. If there characteristic is different, they place it on a different spot on the wall.
    b. The group finds patterns and then gets back into their pairs. (3 minutes)

Part 2

Getting to the Root - Root Cause Analysis (15 minutes)
1. Team leader says, "Of the patterns that we have noticed that seem to have a promising connection to impact, pick the one patterns and brainstorm all of the reasons that it might have impact on the trajectory of the lesson and the learning.
    a. Each pair picks one pattern and writes it in the center of top box of the "Get To The Root" of Impact - Root Cause Tool and brainstorms as many ideas as they can for two minutes.
2. Team leader tells the group to select two of these reasons that they feel are the most highly connected to impacting the trajectory of the lesson and begin a "Four Why's Protocol" by placing their reason in the top box, and then asking themselves "Why" this pattern is occurring. When they think of the first reason, they ask "Why?" again and keep going lower and lower to get a deeper understanding of why this might be happening for this student.
3. EXAMPLE: Student is not engaging with the content in the class.
    a. *Why?*
        i. Each of the students were able to stay focused on the Socratic circle

PLC 2.0 Toolkit

strategy for the entire duration. *Why?*

    ii.   The students knew exactly what it was they were supposed to do. *Why?*

    iii.   They understood the instructions. *Why?*

    iv.   I used an analogy and gave each group of students only one specific duty.

    v.   REFLECTION/LEARNING: With this strategy, when we give students a specific duty and an analogy to remember instructions, they are more likely to be able to complete the task.

4. This process is repeated for the other promising connection to impact.

5. Each of the groups works through their Four Whys, one pattern at a time until all patterns have been discussed.

Part 3

Reflection (5 minutes)

1. The team leader asks the group to consider future learning plans for the strategy or lesson and says, "Given what we discovered about why we might be observing patterns in our classes, what can we learn to assist us in future learning design."

2. The group discusses their findings, and their "Get To The Root" of Impact - Root Cause Tool are placed on the collaborative team Evidence Wall.

97   *PLC 2.0 Toolkit*

"Surface - Deep - Core" Reflection Tool

Part 1: BRAINSTORM - As many ideas as you can as to why you think a strategy worked (or did not work) in your class. Think of things like what you were doing and demonstrating, the activities and tasks, key phrases, timings, set up of the room, student groupings, or anything you feel had an effect. Do this first individually, and then as a group. (7 minutes)

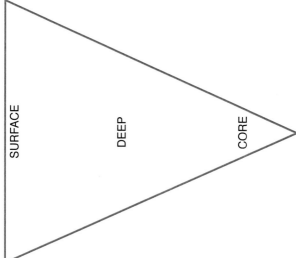

Part 2: LINK - As a team, determine which reasons were less linked to the impact and write them closer to the 'surface'. Determine which were more linked to impact and place them closer to the 'core'. Then draw lines between the ideas that are connected and generate 'linking sentences' to describe the links that the group has made. (15 minutes)

LINKING SENTENCES:

Part 3: THINK - Which sentences and phrases resonate the most with the group? Think of two actions that that the group will DO as a result of the learning and one thing they would DO DIFFERENTLY as a result of the group thinking on this strategy.

ACTION #1:

ACTION #2:

DO DIFFERENTLY:

PLC 2.0 Toolkit

©FIRST EDUCATIONAL RESOURCES 2019

Surface, Deep, Core Reflection Tool

This tool helps teams "lock in the learning" by de-briefing causes that led to the success (or lack of success) of a particular strategy, approach or task.

Prep time: 5 mins to gather materials

Time for Activity: 45 mins

Use this protocol to have your collaborative team:
- work together and come to consensus .
- to analyze on why a particular task or assessment was (or was not) successful in meeting the anticipated level of impact.
- to "keep the learning" and come up with an action plan that leverages the learning from the approach or task in the classroom that can be used in future instructional design.

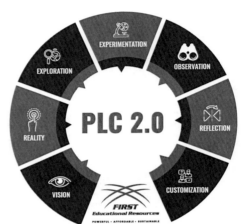

Things You Will Need:
- copies of the 'Surface Deep Core Reflection Tool' for each team member
- Post-it notes, chart paper and markers
- a large piece of chart paper or whiteboard with an inverted triangle labelled with "Surface, Deep, Core"

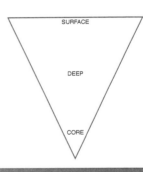

Part 1

Brainstorm (5 minutes)
1. The team leader hands out the 'Surface Deep Core Reflection Tool.'
2. The team leader asks team to individually brainstorm 4-6 reasons why they felt the observed impact of the strategy or approach occurred the way it did in the classroom. Team members are encouraged to be specific in terms of what they or their students were doing or demonstrating that might have contributed to the observed level of impact.
    a. These are written on sticky notes.

3. The team discusses the reasons as a larger group, and tries to make them specific and descriptive, saying things like "That sounds important--what did you see that made you think that?" in order to provide clarity to each sticky note.

Part 2

From Surface to Core (10 minutes)
1. The team leader asks the group to move to the chart paper or white board and individually place their stickies on the inverted triangle diagram--the ones that they felt were highly connected to the level of impact are placed toward the 'core', the ones that were more loosely connected to the impact are placed nearer the 'surface'.
   a. The group discusses the placement of the stickies, asking things like "Can we agree that this one was a bit more 'surface'?" and respectfully challenging the placements so that the diagram represents the thoughts of the team.

Part 3

Creating Connections (10 minutes)
1. Team leader then hands out markers to a few of the team members, and asks them to start to draw lines between ideas that are connected from the core to the deep to the surface elements.
2. Once the team has made connections, the team leader asks the group to make 'linking sentences' out of the connected ideas.
   a. These sentences are written on a separate piece of chart paper.

Part 4

Next Steps - Locking in the Learning (10 minutes)
1. Team leader asks the team "Which phrases resonate with us?" and "What can we learn from these sentences in terms of DO's and DO DIFFERENTLY's when it comes to this approach or task in our classrooms?
2. Team leader reminds the group that regardless of whether something goes as planned or not as planned there is much to be learned--and if we don't reflect upon it immediately, the learning can be lost.
   a. Goal is for the team to generate two actions they will take as a result of the learning and something that they would do differently with this strategy, task or approach in the future.
3. The completed 'Surface, Deep, Core Reflection Tool' is added to the Evidence Wall for the collaborative team.

PLC 2.0 Toolkit

Strategy Review

Department/Collaborative Team: _____ Grade Level/Grouping/Subject (IE. Grade 6 math): _____

PRE-STRATEGY ACTION STATEMENT: What we HOPED to see our students DOING and DEMONSTRATING as a result of this strategy/approach

OVERALL SUMMARY: What we actually saw our students DOING and DEMONSTRATING as a result of this strategy/approach

ATTRIBUTE-RELATED IMPACT OBSERVED BY OUR TEAM

ATTRIBUTE	OBSERVED IMPACT RELATIVE TO ACTION STATEMENT
Attribute: _____	Low |----|----|----|----| High
Attribute: _____	Low |----|----|----|----| High
Attribute: _____	Low |----|----|----|----| High

TIPS AND TEACHING STRATEGIES TO INCREASE IMPACT:

HELPFUL TIPS

PITFALLS TO AVOID:

TEAM MEMBER(S) WHO CAN HELP:

OUR TEAM OVERALL IMPACT / EASE OF IMPLEMENTATION RATING FOR THIS STRATEGY

OVERALL IMPACT — HIGHER

EASE OF IMPLEMENTATION — EASIER

©FIRST EDUCATIONAL RESOURCES 2019

PLC 2.0 Toolkit

Strategy Review

This tool creates a departmental, "Trip Advisor-style" review of a strategy or approach to consolidate the team observations and learning from an impact cycle.

Prep time: 10 minutes to
- photocopy Strategy Review Tool for each team member
- locate the Professional Learning for Observable Impact Tool used for the strategy
- locate the Observation to Impact Connection Tool (TEAM) for the strategy with team observation patterns
- find blank cue cards for each team member

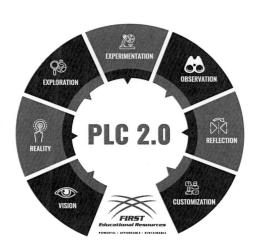

Time for Activity: 40 mins

Use this protocol to have your collaborative team:
- consolidate their learning about a new approach or strategy with a focus on impact in context.
- create a department-based review of the approach or strategy with a guide to tips and pitfalls for ease of future reference for the team or other collaborative teams.

Things You Will Need:
- a copy of the Strategy Review Tool for each team member, with one as the "master copy"
- a copy of the pre-strategy Action Statement that was used prior to trying the new strategy or approach to prepare for impact (from the Professional Learning for Observable Impact Tool used for the strategy)
- a copy of the Observation to Impact Connection Tool (TEAM) for the team
- cue cards, pens

Part 1

Summarizing the Action Statement (15 minutes)
1. Team leader begins by welcoming the group, and setting the stage for the discussion:
   a. "The purpose of today's meeting is for us to consolidate our learning about <the strategy> that we have tried in our classes as a collaborative team over

the last couple of weeks. Our goal is to create a review of <the strategy> by answering the following question: 'Did this strategy have the observable impact that we had hoped for on the instructional challenge that we were facing as a team?'"

2. The team leader brings forward the Action Statement from the Professional Learning for Observable Impact Tool developed prior to learning about the new strategy.

   a. The team has a brief discussion about what they had hoped that they would have observed students doing and demonstrating as a result of this strategy, and what they hoped they would have been doing and demonstrating as a result of the strategy.

   b. *EXAMPLE: Number talks to develop critical thinking for Grade 6 math*

      i. *"We would hear each of the students in the group discussing different aspects of the word problem."*

      ii. *"We would hear students justifying the methods they are using to try to solve the problem."*

      iii. *"We would hear students saying things like, 'I like that method because of …' and 'I hadn't thought of that strategy before.'"*

      iv. *"We would hope to see groups of students writing multiple methods to solve the problem on the white boards."*

      v. *"We would see students making multiple attempts at the problem."*

   c. This is recorded on the Strategy Review page in the Pre-Action Strategy Statement box.

3. The team leader then brings forward the patterns from the "When … then …" statements that were surfaced by the team after the observation cycle and says to the team:

   a. "If someone asked our collaborative team, 'What was the observable impact of this strategy, and how do you know?' how would we respond to them? What would be our 30 second 'elevator speech'?"

      i. The team leader reminds the team to be specific in their elevator pitch, and refer back to the "When … then …" patterns that were high impact or low impact to support their statement.

   b. The team takes three minutes to individually reflect on the patterns and writes their elevator speech on a cue card.

4. Each team member reads their elevator pitch aloud, and the team leader helps the team to create a collaborative summary statement.

   a. *"When we tried the number talks strategy for our intermediate math students, we noticed that students were able to have conversations with their peers about word problems and come up with multiple solutions. We noticed that were able to give each other feedback on which strategies they felt were most effective, but*

103   *PLC 2.0 Toolkit*

they struggled to support their choice of strategy."

    b. This strategy is recorded in the Overall Summary box on the Strategy Review Tool.

Part 2

Creating the Review (10 minutes)

1. Team leader asks the group to focus on Pre-Strategy Action statement and consider the impact that this strategy had on that statement.
   a. The attribute(s) that comprised the primary focus of the strategy (ie. critical thinking for Grade 6 math) is recorded at the top of the "Attribute Related Impact Observed by our Team" box.
      i. OPTION: If the team chooses to include 1-2 other attributes from the school vision that were observed when using strategy, they can be written underneath 'critical thinking for Grade 6 math.'
2. Each team member is asked to consider using an X to mark the slider in terms of level of impact that this strategy had on the attribute in question according to the Action Statement.
   a. The team leader says, "Considering our focus on <critical thinking in our Grade 6 math classes>, how would we assess the impact that this strategy had?"
   b. The team members use observation data to support their choice and come to consensus on where the slider on the Strategy Review Master should go with the rest of the team.
   c. OPTION: This process is repeated for other any attributes listed by the team.
3. The team comes to a consensus on the level of impact, and the Team Leader puts the 'X' in the appropriate spot on the slider on the master Strategy Review document.

Part 3

Future Learning (15 minutes)

1. The team leader then asks the group to consider the strategy and the patterns that they found, and asks, "If someone new or in another collaborative team wanted to try this, what would we tell them were 'must-do's? What are the tips and teaching moves that might make this strategy better?"
2. The team repeats this for pitfalls to avoid.
3. The team leader then asks for support from the group—"If someone wanted to learn a bit more about this strategy and how it might apply to their context, who would be willing to be a contact for our team?"
4. The team leader then asks, "Was this strategy easy or challenging to implement? If

PLC 2.0 Toolkit

someone who had never done this strategy was to attempt it, how would we rate it for ease of implementation?" This process is repeated for 'ease of implementation'.

    a. Each team member is then asked to give an 'overall' ease of implementation review from 1-5 stars (5 being easiest to implement).

        i. The number of stars for the group is reached by consensus, or average if needed.

        ii. The stars are colored in on the master sheet.

5. Each team member is then asked to give an 'overall' impact review from 1-5 stars (5 being highest impact).

    a. The number of stars for the group is reached by consensus, or average if needed.

    b. The stars are colored in on the master sheet.

6. The Strategy Review is then placed on the Evidence Wall for future reference.

"In Their Shoes" Protocol

SECTION 1: OUR LEARNER – What do we know about this learner? What are their strengths?

Student Name:

Course/Grade/Level/Subject:

Considering the Vision of a Learner at our school, what are this student's strengths? When and where do we observe them demonstrating these strengths?

Who are two adults in our school that have a positive connection to this student that we might be able to learn from?

What patterns are we observing with this student in our context?

SECTION 2: GETTING TO THE ROOT – Of the patterns above, select two patterns that would significantly assist this student in moving them forward if they could be changed. Place each of the patterns in the box below, then ask "Why do we think this is happening?". Repeat 5x to get to the root and inspire ideas for a next course of action for the team.

Pattern #1: _____   Pattern #2: _____

WHY?   WHY?
WHY?   WHY?
WHY?   WHY?
WHY?   WHY?
WHY?   WHY?

"ROOT"

SECTION 3: WALKING A MILE "IN THEIR SHOES" – Given what we know about the learner and some of the reasons why we might be observing patterns in our classes, what can we learn to assist us in future designs of approaches to learning, activities and assessments that best meet this student's needs?

PLC 2.0 Toolkit

In Their Shoes Protocol

This tool helps teams take an empathetic, student-centered approach to designing customized learning for students.

Prep time: 2 mins to photocopy protocol

Time for Activity: 30-40 minutes

Use this protocol to have your collaborative team:
- engage in a collaborative, empathy-based conversation that helps them see through the eyes of a learner in their context.
- to talk about their individual students or discuss a single student as a group.

Things You Will Need:
- copies of the In Their Shoes Protocol for each participant
- (OPTIONAL) copies of the Departmental/Team Level Vision of a Learner and School Vision of a Learner.

Part 1

Setting The Stage (2 minutes)
1. Team leader starts by saying "Today we are going to be considering a student in your context that you might be struggling to move forward in your classes. We say 'push forward' because we know that students that are coasting can be just as disengaged and need as much support as those who are struggling, and we need to ensure all of our learners are moving forward. This protocol gives us the opportunity to 'walk a mile in their shoes' in order for us to create a customized approach to their learning."
2. Team leader provides the 'In Their ShoesTool', and asks team members to consider a student that they want to move forward in their classes.

Part 2

Getting to know the student (5-7 minutes)
1. Team leader reminds the team that this is going to be a strengths-based discussion, and that we want to speak of the child in a way that is supportive.

a. "How a grandmother would speak of their grandchild."
2. If available, the team leader passes out copies of the Departmental/Team Level Vision of a Learner and School Vision of a Learner, and asks the team to use this as a lens to consider strengths that the student has demonstrated, and the context where they demonstrate these strengths
    a. "Where are the places where this student demonstrates strengths, and what can we learn from that context?"
3. Team leader refers to the Vision of a Learner, and Team leader asks the group to consider who two staff members might be at the school who have a connection with a child
    a. If they are not aware of two staff members, team considers who might be able to help them find out this information (guidance counselors, administration).
4. The individuals then begin to brainstorm some of the patterns that they are observing from the student.
    a. These could range from 'attendance' and 'engagement issues' to students who 'complete all of their work before the rest of the class' and 'frequently seem bored or unchallenged'.
    b. This tool is for students on all parts of the learning continuum.

Part 3

Getting to the Root - Root Cause Analysis (15-20 minutes)
1. Team leader says "Of the patterns that you have noticed, pick the two patterns that, if you were able to change those patterns, would make a significant difference to the learning trajectory of the student."
    a. Team picks two patterns, and writes them in the appropriate boxes on the 'In Their Shoes Tool'.
2. Team leader then asks the team to get into pairs or threes and work on one of the team members patterns at a time in order to have 'other sets of eyes' on the pattern.
    a. If the team is discussing an individual student, the whole group is involved in this stage.
3. Team leader tells the group that they are going to go deep into the problem using the "5 Why's Protocol" by placing their reason in the top box, and then asking themselves "Why" this pattern is occurring. When they think of the first reason, they ask "Why?" again, and keep going lower and lower to get a deeper understanding of why this might be happening for this student.
4. EXAMPLE: student is not engaging with the content in the class
    a. *Why?*
        i. The student is not interested in the material. *Why?*

PLC 2.0 Toolkit   *108*

      ii.   The student the material might not be connected to their context. *Why?*

      iii.   We are not sure what the student's context is? *Why?*

      iv.   We have not connected with the student in a way where they feel they can tell us their context. *Why?*

      v.   We have been busy with the rest of the class.

      vi.   ACTION: We need to make time to connect with this student so we can determine their context and then begin to connect our content in a way that is meaningful to them.

5. Each of the groups works through their 5 Whys, one pattern at a time until all patterns have been discussed.

Part 4

Walking a Mile "In Their Shoes" (10 minutes)

1. The team leader asks the group to consider future learning plans for the student, and says "Given what we know about the learner and some of the reasons why we might be observing patterns in our classes, what can we learn to assist us in future designs of approaches to learning, activities and assessments that best meet this student's needs?"

    a. The team leader encourages team members by saying things like "If we were in this student's shoes, what would we want our teachers to do to help us take the first steps in moving forward?"

2. Team members begin to make plans, and then share out to the rest of the group what they have learned about the student in the process, and what approaches they are going to take in the future to customize the learning for the student.

Individual Customization Plan - STUDENT

SECTION 1: OUR LEARNER - What do we know about this learner?

Student Name:

Who are two adults in our school that have a positive connection to this student that we might be able to learn from?

Course/Grade/Level/Subject:

Considering the Vision of a Learner at our school, what are this student's strengths? When and where do we observe them demonstrating these strengths?

Consider this learner in our context and when the learner is MOST engaged: "This learner learns best when they are _____"

What is the PRIOR KNOWLEDGE and PRIOR ATTITUDES of this students about this topic? How do we know? What (other) actions do we need to take to find out?

LEARNING DESIGN FRAMING QUESTION: "How might we design learning for a student who is <list strengths>, who learns best when they are <list characteristics>, and has prior knowledge in <list knowledge> and prior attitudes of <list attitudes>?"

SECTION 2: THEIR LEARNING - What do we need to be demonstrated below.

OUTCOMES/TASKS: List the tasks or outcomes yet to be demonstrated below. Then plot the corresponding number on the Customization Graph Below on the next page.

1.

2.

3.

4.

PLC 2.0 Toolkit

©FIRST EDUCATIONAL RESOURCES 2019

110

SECTION 3: OUR LEARNING
Plot the outcomes we need the learner to demonstrate on the graph below to determine the level of customization required.

Student Connection Factor
(How well does the task match the student's capability AND motivation to do this task)

"I don't want to do this."
OR
"I can't do this."

LOW

"I can do this, and I want to do this, I just haven't yet"

HIGH

"Lower Priority Tasks" — Less connected to our Vision and less critical to success in this subject area

"Higher Priority Tasks" — Highly connected to our Vision AND critical to success in this subject area

INCREASED NEED FOR CUSTOMIZATION

Activity A

Activity B

ENGAGEMENT BOOSTER - How might we make this even more relevant to our learner?

CONNECTIVITY FACTOR (I want to do this!)

- ○ Connects to their prior learning
- ○ The learner it needs now, or in the near future
- ○ Makes something easier/saves the learner time
- ○ Relates to something the learner is already doing
- ○ Impacts something that is important to the learner
- ○ Provides feedback to the learner

ACCOUNTABILITY FACTOR ("I need to do this!")

- ○ Requires thinking to be made visible
- ○ Requires conversation
- ○ Requires creation of a product
- ○ Requires iteration of the product
- ○ Requires presentation of the product
- ○ Requires utilization of the product

ACCESSIBILITY FACTOR ("I can do this!")

- ○ Learner-friendly language
- ○ Concepts chunked into manageable bits
- ○ Connects to the learner through analogy/story
- ○ Utilizes familiar images/symbols/patterns
- ○ Allows for self-pacing and mastery
- ○ Allows for voice and choice

©FIRST EDUCATIONAL RESOURCES 2019

111

PLC 2.0 Toolkit

SECTION 4: OUR DESIGN - Brainstorm the ideas to increase the customization of the tasks or outcomes to best meet the needs of your learner in the space below

LEARNING DESIGN FRAMING QUESTION: "How might we design learning for a student who is <list strengths>, who learns best when they are <list characteristics>, and has prior knowledge in <list knowledge> and prior attitudes of <list attitudes>?"

ACTIVITY/ASSESSMENT/OUTCOME #1: _____

We can increase the CONNECTIVITY FACTOR of this outcome/task for this student by…	We can increase the ACCESSIBILITY FACTOR of this outcome/task for this student by…	We can increase the ACCOUNTABILITY FACTOR of this outcome/task for this student by…	Date For Completion

ACTIVITY/ASSESSMENT/OUTCOME #2: _____

We can increase the CONNECTIVITY FACTOR of this outcome/task for this student by…	We can increase the ACCESSIBILITY FACTOR of this outcome/task for this student by…	We can increase the ACCOUNTABILITY FACTOR of this outcome/task for this student by…	Date For Completion

PLC 2.0 Toolkit

©FIRST EDUCATIONAL RESOURCES 2019

SECTION 4 (CONTINUED): OUR DESIGN

Brainstorm the ideas to increase the customization of the tasks or outcomes to best meet the needs of your learner in the space below

LEARNING DESIGN FRAMING QUESTION: "How might we design learning for a student who is <list characteristics>, and has prior knowledge in <list knowledge> and prior attitudes of <list attitudes>?"

ACTIVITY/ASSESSMENT/OUTCOME #3: _____

We can increase the CONNECTIVITY FACTOR of this outcome/task for this student by…	We can increase the ACCESSIBILITY FACTOR of this outcome/task for this student by…	We can increase the ACCOUNTABILITY FACTOR of this outcome/task for this student by…	Date For Completion

ACTIVITY/ASSESSMENT/OUTCOME #4: _____

We can increase the CONNECTIVITY FACTOR of this outcome/task for this student by…	We can increase the ACCESSIBILITY FACTOR of this outcome/task for this student by…	We can increase the ACCOUNTABILITY FACTOR of this outcome/task for this student by…	Date For Completion

PLC 2.0 Toolkit

Individual Customization Plan

This tool helps collaborative teams design a strengths-based, customized action plan to engage a learner in high-priority tasks.

Prep time: 2 mins to photocopy protocol

Time for Activity: 60 minutes

Use this protocol to have your collaborative team:
- engage in an strengths-based conversation about a student who is having challenges completing high priority tasks.
- increase the engagement factor of high priority tasks for the student through the lenses of connection, accessibility and accountability.
- create an action plan that empowers the student to demonstrate high priority outcomes.

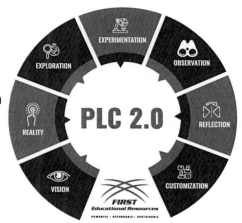

Things You Will Need:
- copies of the Individual Customization Plan template for each participant
- a list of high priority activities/assessments that the student has yet to do and demonstrate
- copies of the Departmental/Team Level Vision of a Learner and School Vision of a Learner

Part 1

Setting The Stage (2 minutes)
1. Team leader starts by saying
    a. "Today we are going to be considering a student that we are struggling to move forward in our classes."
    b. "Right now, regardless of whether we believe that this student 'cannot' do and demonstrate the outcomes that will allow them to be successful or 'will not' do or demonstrate those outcomes doesn't matter: what we know is they 'ARE NOT' doing these outcomes."
    c. We need to create a customized support plan that meets them <u>where they are at</u> and gets them where we want them to be. Today, we will be looking at this student's strengths and how they learn best so that by the end of our time

PLC 2.0 Toolkit   *114*

together, we will leave with a support plan that meets their needs."

2. Team leader provides copies of the Individual Customization Plan template for each participant, and asks the team to make sure that they have any activities or assessments that will allow us to observe the learning we need from the student handy for later in the discussion.

Part 2

Getting to Know Our Learner (10 minutes)

1. Team leader refers to the Vision of a Learner, and Team leader asks the group to consider who two staff members might be at the school who have a connection with a child
   a. If they are not aware of two staff members, team considers who might be able to help them find out this information (guidance counselors, administration)
2. If available, the team leader passes out copies of the Departmental/Team Level Vision of a Learner and School Vision of a Learner, and asks the team to use this as a lens to consider strengths that the student has demonstrated, and the context where they demonstrate these strengths. (5 minutes)
   a. "Where are the places where this student demonstrates strengths, and what can we learn from that context?"
   b. Team reflects on in-class and outside of class situations, and team leader encourages the group to assume the best intentions of the learner, and to take a curious approach to what they are observing, using the phrase "I wonder..."
      i. "He's loud" can become "I wonder how we could look at ways for him to demonstrate these outcomes where he gets to use his voice?"
      ii. "She hands assignments in late." can become "I wonder what things make her want to be punctual?"
   c. The team leader encourages the team to come up with at least 5 specific strengths of the student, and these are filled into the form.
      i. The team does not leave this section until these specific strengths are filled in.
3. The team builds on the strengths, and the team leader asks the collaborative team to consider when they see the student most engaged, and asks "How does this student learn best?"
   a. Types of activities and assessments are considered.
4. The team then begins to brainstorm the prior knowledge of the student that could connect to the material yet to be demonstrated.
   a. This could come from the collaborative team area, or from other areas where the student has demonstrated strengths or attributes

5. The "Our learner" section is completed with a LEARNING DESIGN FRAMING QUESTION from the team leader that is framed using the following stem:
   a. "How might we design learning for a student who is <list strengths>, who learns best when they are <list characteristics>, and has prior knowledge in <list knowledge> and prior attitudes of <list attitudes>?
   b. NOTE: This step is crucial and must not be skipped. It is the guiding question that will shape the plan and ensure that the collaborative team is considering the needs of the student.

Part 3

Their Learning (5 minutes)
1. The team leader asks the team to bring forward activities or assessments of high priority outcomes that we have yet to observe the student do or demonstrate.
2. The team leader asks the collaborative team to begin to consider the outstanding activities or assessments and consider the following question:
   a. "If we truly want this student to engage in these activities or assessments, how might we look at this task through the lens of the learning design framing question outlined in Section 3?"
   b. The team takes 3 minutes to silently and individually reflect on the activities in front of them.

Part 4

Our Learning (10 minutes)
1. The team leader asks the group to refer to the diagram in Section 3.

PLC 2.0 Toolkit

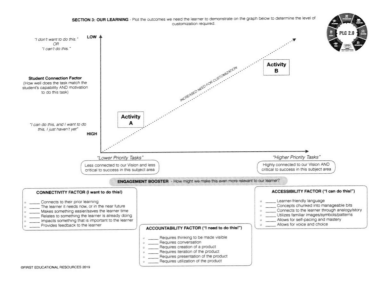

2. The team leader asks the group to consider each of the activities or assessments that the student has yet to do or demonstrate, and to place them on individual Post-It note.
3. The team discusses each task to determine the level of customization that is likely going to be required for the student to be successful in demonstrating the activity or assessment through two lenses:
    a. The level of student connection (the match to student capability and motivation to do the task).
    b. The level of importance to the success of the student.
        i. HIGH LEVEL OF CUSTOMIZATION: A task that is highly critical for student success but has a low connection to the student (for reasons of ability OR motivation) would be placed <u>higher and to the right.</u>
            1. Example: a lengthy and complex chemistry lab and write up
        ii. LOW LEVEL OF CUSTOMIZATION: A task that is less critical to student success and is easily connected to to student ability or motivation.
            1. Example: the final iteration of a persuasive letter to the editor
    c. The team places the Post-It notes with each of the activities or assessments on the diagram.

Part 5

Our Design: Task Customization (20-40 minutes, depending on number of activities)
1. The team leader asks the team to consider the task that will require the most customization first. This is written in the ACTIVITY/ASSESSMENT/OUTCOME line.
2. The team then looks at the activity/assessment through the three lenses of CONNECTIVITY, ACCESSIBILITY and ACCOUNTABILITY using the Engagement Booster.
    a. The team looks at each of the ways these factors can be increased for this

individual student, based upon the LEARNING DESIGN FRAMING QUESTION developed in Part 2:

    i. "How might we design learning for a student who is \<list strengths\>, who learns best when they are \<list characteristics\>, and has prior knowledge in \<list knowledge\> and prior attitudes of \<list attitudes\>?

3. The team leader encourages the collaborative team to keep the student at the center the customization of each task.
4. Once the new task design has been created, it is compared to the Learning Design Framing Question to see how well it matches the learner profile.
5. Each activity is also given a completion date, which is based upon the Accessibility and Accountability Factors.
6. This process is repeated for each of the tasks that the team has put forward.

Part 6

Reflection (5 minutes)

1. The team leader asks the group to consider the student, and discuss this reflection question:

    a. What is most important for this student? Is it making learning relevant for them, making learning accessible for them, or holding them accountable for their learning? Did we reflect that in our design?

Organizational Assessment Tool

School: _____ Date: _____ This is our _____ Organizational Assessment

PLC 2.0 Element	Where we are at / What's going well	Where we need to go	Our Next Step	Priority
Observable Vision We have a Vision of a Learner that has been co-designed by our community that details what we would be doing and demonstrating, the tasks and outcomes that connect our teaching and assessments to our vision.				○ High ○ Med ○ Low
Evidence-based Reality We have examined our tasks, instructional practices, and assessments through the lens of our Vision of a Learner to determine the gaps and our instructional challenges.				○ High ○ Med ○ Low
Exploration We have determined promising instructional strategies to co-create an Action Statement that is connected to and accessible by our educators and holds us accountable to each other through making our learning observable.				○ High ○ Med ○ Low
Experimentation and Observation We have determined high priority outcomes, created the structures that enable us to collaboratively design engaging learning experiences, and objectively observe through self or peer observations in our classrooms.				○ High ○ Med ○ Low
Reflection We individually and collaboratively reflect upon our tasks and teaching that leads to establish patterns that connect our actions to the specific student outputs in our Action Statement.				○ High ○ Med ○ Low
Customization We have mechanisms to make the products of learning for our learners (students AND educators) visible to enable us to create developmental learning plans with multiple entry points that meet our learners where the are at.				○ High ○ Med ○ Low

119 PLC 2.0 Toolkit

Organizational Assessment Tool - Tracking Our Progress

Use this form to track your progress in each of the areas of the PLC 2.0 model using at least three dates over the course of the year that your collaborative group, department or school have made towards moving from vision to impact.

DATE	Observable Vision	Evidence-Based Reality	Exploration	Experimentation and Observation	Reflection	Customization
	We have a Vision of a Learner that has been co-designed by our community that details what we would be doing and demonstrating, the tasks and outcomes that connect our teaching and assessments to our vision.	We have examined our tasks, instructional practices, and assessments through the lens of our Vision of a Learner to determine the gaps and our instructional challenges.	We have determined promising instructional strategies to co-create an Action Statement that is connected to and accessible by our educators and holds us accountable to each other through making our learning observable.	We have determined high priority outcomes, created the structures that enable us to collaboratively design engaging learning experiences, and objectively observe through self or peer observations in our classrooms.	We individually and collaboratively reflect upon our tasks and teaching that leads to establish patterns that connect our actions to the specific student outputs in our Action Statement.	We have mechanisms to make the products of learning for our learners (students AND educators) visible to enable us to create developmental learning plans with multiple entry points that meet our learners where the are at.
EXCEEDING						
ON TRACK						
EMERGING						
BASELINE						

PLC 2.0 Toolkit

Organizational Assessment Tool

This tool helps school leaders and collaborative teams to develop a baseline and track progress in each of the PLC 2.0 elements.

Prep time: 5-10 mins to gather supplies, find and label chart paper and gather cue cards and markers.

Time for Activity: 45-65 mins

Use this protocol to have your collaborative team or staff:
- take a strengths-based approach to progress that has been made in each of the elements of the PLC 2.0 model.
- to determine higher, medium and lower priorities and next steps on the PLC 2.0 journey.

Things You Will Need:
- 6 cue cards per participant, post-it notes, markers, timer
- groups of 2-4
- copies of the 'Organizational Assessment Tool' for each participant and copies of copy of the 'Organizational Assessment Tool - Tracking Our Progress'
- 6 large pieces of chart paper set up as below, one for each PLC 2.0 focus:
  - Observable Vision
  - Evidence-based Reality
  - Exploration
  - Experimentation and Observation
  - Reflection
  - Customization

Where we are at / What's going well	PLC 2.0 Element	Where we need to go	Our Next Step	Priority
	Observable Vision			

Part 1

"What are we noticing?" - Reflecting on what's going well, and where we need to go

1. The team leader hands out 'Organizational Assessment Tool' handout, and asks the group to read through each of the six PLC 2.0 elements.
2. The team leader describes the tool, which is in the format of a single-column rubric.
   a. Single-column rubrics are used to work from our strengths (What's gone well) as well as to determine our areas of growth (Where we need to go) so that we can begin to prioritize our first and next steps going forward.
3. The team leader asks participants to individually fill out the 'What's gone well' column. If the school has yet to get started in that particular area, the team leader reassures the group that it's totally fine! They ask the group to consider things that are happening in the school that might help to get this part of the PLC 2.0 model started. (6 minutes)
4. The team leader asks each participant to take the 'What's gone well' for each element that they feel is most important and write-it on a Post-It note. (2 minutes)
5. Participants take each of their Post-It notes and place it under the 'What's gone well' on the large pieces of chart paper for each element area. Participants are then asked to gallery walk around the room using the prompt "What are we noticing?" from the team leader to get a sense of the thoughts of the larger group. A larger group discussion is prompted, and other group members ask things like 'What are we observing that makes us think this?'. (7 minutes)
6. This process is repeated for "Where we need to go." (15 minutes, same timings as above)

PLC 2.0 Toolkit

Part 2

Considering Future Directions (5 minutes)

1. After the group has reflected on strengths and where they need to go, the team leader tells group "Now that we've heard our strengths and where we might need to go to move us forward, we need to prioritize! We can't do it all at once, so we need to decide on which of the elements are our highest priorities. Given the strengths and where we need to go, which elements would we call 'high priority', 'medium priority' and 'low priority'?
   a. Going one by one through each element, the team leader asks team members to hold up one finger (pointer please!) for high priority, two fingers for 'middle' and three fingers for those elements that are lower priority.
      i. The 'high priority' element charts are brought to the front of the group.

Part 3

Strategy Shuffle (8-10 minutes/strategy)

1. For each 'high priority element':
   a. team leader asks group to consider all that they have heard and come up with their 'best idea' for a "Next Step" in that PLC 2.0 element area: they write this strategy and the element area on a cue card.
   b. The group then stands and does a 'strategy shuffle' - the team leader asks each group member to stand with their cue card, and move around the room exchanging cards with one member, then another and another until the team leader says 'Stop!'
      i. The group member looks at the strategy, and places a ranking of 1 to 4 on the back.
         1. 1 means the idea is perhaps a 'not yet', a 4 means "let's do this!"
      ii. This 'strategy shuffle' is repeated 4 times, the ideas are scored, and the ones with the highest total scores are elevated to the top of the priority list to create a roadmap for next steps.
         1. Participants are asked to consider how they would score the strategy prior to turning over the card and seeing how it has been previously scored.
   c. This process is repeated if there is another high priority.

123   *PLC 2.0 Toolkit*

Part 4

Reflect (2 minutes)

1. The team leader asks the groups to create a statement using an "I used to think...now I think" protocol, and asks for the group to share their thoughts about the process.

Part 5

Check (5 minutes)

1. The team leader asks the group for dates and commitments to next steps, and places these on the large poster to be kept as visible in the collaborative area.
   (3 minutes)
2. The team leader hands out a copy of the 'Organizational Assessment Tool - Tracking Our Progress', and asks each team member to write today's date in the 'baseline' column at the bottom of the tool, and to assess whether the team is emerging, 'on track' or 'exceeding.'
3. The team sets a date to revisit these forms to determine if progress has been made to the elements of the PLC 2.0 model.
4. The master 'Organizational Assessment Tool' goes on the Evidence Wall for the collaborative team, as does each copy of the 'Organizational Assessment Tool - Tracking Our Progress' from the team.

PLC 2.0 Toolkit